Cedric Robinson
The Queen's Guide to the Sands

Time and Tide

GOLDEN YEARS ON MORECAMBE BAY

50

GREAT NORTHERN

Great Northern Books
PO Box 213, Ilkley, LS29 9WS
www.greatnorthernbooks.co.uk

ISBN: 978 0 9572951 6 2

Design and layout: David Burrill

Printed in India

CIP Data
A catalogue for this book is available from the British Library

Acknowledgements

I owe a special thanks to David Joy, who with his wife Judith found time to visit Guides Farm and suggest that I write this book. I am also especially indebted to Sir Chris Bonington, who so kindly wrote the Foreword. I am very moved by the articles and letters that form the second half of this book and would like to thank all contributors. I am only sorry that it has not been possible to include all the letters received. A personal thanks to Mrs Jane Keelan, for long and enduring patience in carefully reading through my manuscript, and, from my scribble, making an excellent job of it.

I am most grateful to everyone who provided photographs. My son Paul went out onto the sands with me in the coldest of weather to take pictures. Ian Hughes accompanied me out in the Bay on several occasions with his camera. Tania Callagher of the University of Central Lancashire kindly provided the photos taken by Neil Stanley. Similarly, James Thurlow helpfully supplied the pictures of the cross-Bay run taken by James Kirby.

I also thank Phyllis Capstick, who has been so involved in the horse rides across the Bay, and Ted Smith of the Ribble Valley Driving Club.

Title page photo by Ian Hughes

Contents

Foreword

Sir Chris Bonington

Exploring and climbing mountains in all corners of the world is a wonderful experience but crossing the Morecambe Bay sands with Cedric Robinson is something else. I did so for the first time in the summer of 2012 – and it was a day I shall never forget.

The occasion was a Bay Walk in which four charities participated. One of the four was the Friends of the Lake District and I was there as a Vice President. We had some 120 members and supporters and we raised over £2,000. I can well understand why the Friends hope that crossing the Bay will become a more regular event in their calendar.

For almost forty years I have lived in Cumbria just below High Pike, the north-east bastion of the Northern Fells. I've climbed it a thousand times and never cease to wonder at the beauty of the view from its summit, revelling in the belief that there is nowhere in the world more beautiful than the Lake District.

It is easy to forget that Morecambe Bay on the southern edge of the county provides a final flourish that is utterly different but still deeply inspiring. This is 'big sky' country with its 120 square miles of mudflats and sand – the largest such expanse in Britain. It is a glorious place for wading birds, magnificent sunsets and often simply the sound of silence.

While mountain peaks change according to the seasons, they certainly don't do so on the same daily basis as the shifting sands of Morecambe Bay. I was full of admiration for Cedric's knowledge of their foibles and quickly realised that here was someone with very special skills. Crossings are becoming both more challenging and more dangerous, in part due to climate change, but Cedric carries such difficulties in his stride. He sets out across the sands at a cracking pace and keeps huge parties in order with blasts of his whistle.

More than 10,000 people a year are now guided across the Bay and the sum that has been raised for worthy charities is immense. Recent participants have included some students, who with admirable precision calculated that Cedric has now walked the equivalent of twice round the world! It is entirely appropriate that in the same year he should celebrate both his 80th birthday and the 50th anniversary of his appointment as Queen's Guide to the Sands. This book is a worthy commemoration of such an achievement.

Opposite: Sir Chris Bonington (right) photographed with
Cedric Robinson when he made his first crossing of the
Morecambe Bay sands. (Friends of the Lake District)

Preface

It has been my privilege to edit almost all the books that Cedric Robinson has written on his beloved Morecambe Bay. This one has given me even greater pleasure than its predecessors, as it celebrates the remarkable 50th anniversary of his appointment as the Queen's Guide to the Sands.

It falls into two distinct sections. In Part 1, Cedric writes about his life on the Bay and the many memorable happenings that have occurred down the years. He both brings the story up-to-date and looks back at events he has never before covered in depth. For the first time he writes fully about the fascinating events of the late 1960s, when he was out in all weathers involved in preparatory work for a proposed Morecambe Bay barrage. He clearly had mixed feelings, as such a project would have ended his role as the Queen's Guide. Happily, it has never happened.

Part 2 is an amazing collective 'thank you', which highlights Cedric's unique human achievements. Writers from many different walks of life praise his knowledge and understanding of the Bay, the way he has raised millions for charities, and his diverse skills as fisherman, farmer, raconteur and gifted speaker.

Devotees of the cross-Bay walk describe how this unique institution has developed and how they love being guided by Cedric 'like the children of Hamelin following the pied piper'! Less familiar are the now regular and exhilarating rides across the Bay on horseback – and riders both capture the magic and praise Cedric for joyfully letting them experience the beauty of the sands. Finally, the Archbishop of Liverpool rounds off these pages with an Afterword, appropriately referring to the wonder of the Bay that Cedric has shared with thousands.

David Joy
Editor

Part 1

50 Golden Years on Morecambe Bay

by Cedric Robinson

Cedric Robinson,
photographed in
December 2012 on the
shores of Morecambe
Bay. (Philip Dunn –
www.photoactive.co.uk)

Olive Robinson – a
recent photograph
taken inside Guides
Farm. (Paul Nickson)

1. 50 Years as Queen's Guide

Morecambe Bay has been described in many ways over the years – 'The lost wilderness in England', 'The wet Sahara' and many more. I myself would describe it as unique – a place on its own.

Many years ago I was asked if I would accompany a small group of people across the Ribble estuary from Southport to Lytham St Annes, which I duly did. In most recent years I have crossed the Duddon estuary from Askam to Millom with a much larger group of people. Although these estuaries can be a danger to the unwary, neither can compare to our Morecambe Bay. It is a landscape like no other, and I think myself privileged to have been a part of it. Firstly as a fisherman and later, for the past 50 years, as 'Queen's Guide to the Sands of Morecambe Bay'.

Like my predecessors, I live at Guides Farm at Kents Bank. Neither my wife Olive nor I are 'spring chickens', but she shares the responsibilities conscientiously. Nowadays the call for my services during the summer months is very demanding.

The tide can advance at the speed of a galloping horse and the dreaded quicksand can take a fisherman's tractor down in seconds. I actually witnessed this many years ago when out at night shrimping. A good friend at that time lost his tractor never to be seen again. The tractor, trailer and nets – the lot went down. The fisherman just had time and the presence of mind to jump clear. This in itself is a frightening thought, but it does not deter the many thousands of people still willing to take part in one or more of the now famous Morecambe Bay Walks.

Weather plays its part in most people's lives but none more so than with the Sands Guide. For the fishermen and me who worked this great expanse of sea and sand, it provided a dangerous and hard living. When I was a youngster leaving school, I only wanted to follow the sands for a living, like my father and my grandfather. Even my grandmother was a fisherwoman. At a young age one can never really see danger and, when lots of fishermen were together on the sands, conversation between them never ever taught me anything.

It was only when my father and I were out on these sands alone that I would begin to ask him questions and take notice of what he had to say to me. He would explain about the dykes and gullies, the channels and the quicksand and how the tide can come around you at what he called 'the meetings'. These are high areas not covered by the tide till the last minute, with the tidal water flooding over the sand from the sides both east and west. Following heavy rainfall, freshwater dykes always had to be watched. All of this information was of interest to me and for my own good and gradually over the years I have come to learn more and more about the sands of Morecambe Bay.

In 1963 I heard that the post of the Queen's Guide to the Sands was becoming available. After discussing this with my wife and young family and my parents, it was a challenge I was willing to take on. I applied and was chosen for the job. Those earlier years out in the Bay, working from a horse and cart in all weathers, night time and day according to the tides, stood me in good stead for the position I now held.

In my first season the walks started from across the Bay at Hest Bank, near to Morecambe, and took us no longer than three hours, coming ashore on the promenade at Grange near to the old swimming pool. Not many people had heard of the Bay walks all those years ago, but with a new guide and lots of publicity, the numbers soon increased to around 150 or more walkers.

On the very first walk – and luckily it was only a small group of walkers – Olive thought it would be polite to invite them back to Guides Farm for a cup of tea. So we did, and they all came into the house, taking their muddy shoes off at the door and piling into the sitting room. They were a splendid group of people, very interested in the history of the sands and the farm, and dear Olive came in with a large pot of tea and biscuits. It was a lovely experience for us all to sit, drink tea and

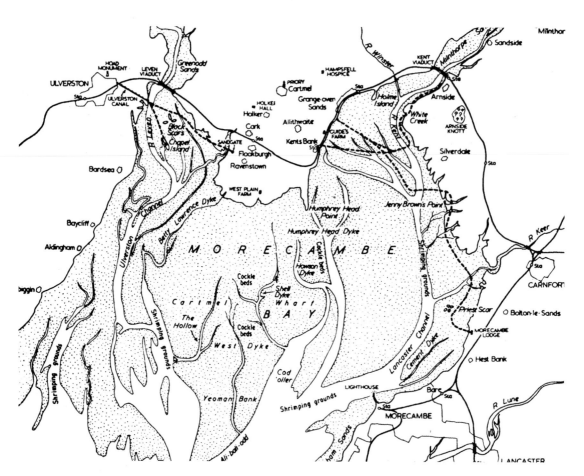

Map of Morecambe Bay, drawn by Olive Robinson, with the routes of the cross-Bay walks shown by dotted lines. The current route heads south from Arnside, close to White Creek, and then swings west to cross the River Kent and head over to Kents Bank.

talk about their walking across the sands of Morecambe Bay.

There was no electricity supply to Guides Farm, so all the enquiries came through the post and had to be answered. This took up a lot of my time, but we came through it with numbers soon increasing. It did take a while to get electricity to the farm and a phone installed, but soon Olive was taking calls for the walks at all times of the day.

We had to keep a record of numbers of people who crossed the Bay, so she would also book down the names and addresses of people and the numbers in each group. Very rarely had I to cancel a walk, I would say probably one in fifty. We seemed to have much better weather, with summers of long days of sunshine and no rain for weeks at a time – or very little. If the weather became hot and sultry, we would experience a thunderstorm, but after that the air would clear and the rain would disappear. Crossing the sands was much easier in those early years, with the rivers Keer and Kent being mostly shallow and practically free from quicksand.

Health & Safety was not a problem and, as far as I know, none of my predecessors took out a public liability insurance, but now that has all changed. Safety guidance has been drawn up by Lancaster City Council and South Lakeland District Council following consultation with HM Coastguard, Police and local operators. This guidance is not a law in itself but provides a minimum benchmark that helps in demonstrating compliance with the duties placed on organisers. Operators are free to adopt alternative approaches, so long as they can demonstrate an equivalent level of safety. My three helpers and myself do not seem to have any problems on that score, although at times there have been worries with other operators coming from the Morecambe side of the Bay.

As the largest inter-tidal area in the United Kingdom, the Bay presents a number of well-documented hazards to the ill prepared and unwary. Weather, tides, quicksand, unpredictable channels, remoteness and the speed of changing conditions all add to the risks.

The recorded history of people walking across Morecambe Bay goes back many centuries. Until the coming of the railway in the 1850s a trek across the sands by foot or horse-drawn carriage was the only way of avoiding the lengthy and poorly maintained coastal road route. In order to reduce the many cases of drowning the first official Guides to the Bay were appointed by the Crown in the 1500s – a practice that continues to this day. Cases of drowning, however, still tragically continue to occur to the inexperienced and unwary. The greatest tragedy in recent times was the death of twenty Chinese workers engaged in cockle gathering in Morecambe Bay on the night of 5th February 2004. It is essential that anyone attempting to walk across the Bay seeks the support of the official Guide.

The safety history of organised walks by me and my helpers is very good. In recent years the popularity of the walks has increased considerably with interest being expressed by different parties and persons in organising and participating in the cross-Bay experience. All those newly enquiring are sent a pack of guidelines by Olive and we hope that these do not deter anyone from coming along and enjoying the experience of a lifetime.

Olive tells me that in 1946 she and five of her friends from the village of Ravenstown, near Flookburgh, crossed the Bay from Hest Bank, to Humphrey Head in safety without a Guide. A very popular paperback was written by a Mr Pope and described the route that could be taken – I think this small book was called *The Sands of Morecambe Bay*. The River Kent was at that time close to the Grange over Sands shore and had been for almost fifty years. They were extremely lucky with low tides and good weather, which was all in their favour.

The magnificent setting of Guides Farm, seen from the back of the house with the broad sweep of Morecambe Bay stretching away into the distance. (John Clegg)

I would not advise anyone to attempt the same crossing today without the company of myself as the Official Guide or a sandgrown person, who would know the sands and the times of the tides. Now, with the unpredictable weather patterns and frequent changes, it would need a miracle for any lay person to cross in safety.

Our weather is changing rapidly and dramatically and this could be something to do with global warming. A few years ago changes were already being noticed. When you met someone the weather patterns were always the topic of conversation. No longer do we have the seasons we can remember – spring, summer, autumn and hard winters with snow, ice and severe frosts. All that has gone to the wind. The rains now come with a vengeance, the like of which we have never seen before, with no let up from stronger winds and higher tides. That is a dangerous combination and brings sudden, dramatic changes, not just in the rivers but to the full extent of the Bay. Vast areas of quicksand can form, where previously it had been safe. Rainwater is much heavier than the sea water and finds its way through the surface of the sands.

The favourite question always put to me by the public is, "Don't you ever get fed up with going out on the sands?" My truthful answer is, "No – not ever!" Each day is a challenge and it is so pleasing when things turn out right. This does not always happen now, with the sudden weather changes and higher tides and strong winds. We do have some disappointments, but you have to take what the Bay gives you and make the best of what you have got.

2. Cross-Bay Walks

Before the walk

A walk across Morecambe Bay in safety could not take place without lots of preparation, which can take us up to four or five hours. The season of 2012 was the wettest spring and summer on record for over 100 years and was especially difficult.

I am a laidback person, but I do take my job very seriously and nothing is left to chance. The sands and the River Kent must be thoroughly checked the day before each walk. On this day, which is usually a Friday prior to the weekend walks, 'brobs' have to be cut from the laurels close to the farm. These branches are put well down into the sand and act as good markers on the route to be taken with the walkers over the next two days. A long heavy crowbar is used and worked down into the sand. This makes way for the laurels and then the sand sets firm around them. In the low areas and on the sides of the River Kent, these 'brobs' serve their purpose over that weekend when the tides are at their lowest. Once they rise up to about seven, eight or nine metres, the power of the incoming and outgoing tide is so strong that it works them out of the sand and washes them away. So before the next weekend when we have walks, the marking out of the routes and the River Kent crossing have to be repeated once again.

Usually on the Thursday, I ring Barry,

Marking the route with 'brobs' – laurel branches cut close to Guides Farm. (Ian Hughes)

Mike and John – my dedicated helpers – to make sure that they know the time we will be leaving Guides Farm the following day and that they will be available. I always make up a flask of milky coffee and John provides the biscuits. All three of them are keen and so interested in the Bay, and I owe them a special thanks for their support.

Instead of taking the Sandpiper trailer, which is quite heavy, just for handiness we use a transport box that is attached to the tractor hydraulics. Farmers use them all the time, so we thought we would do the same, and this does our job quite well and holds all the equipment needed on the day. John makes it quite comfortable to ride on and puts cushions in before leaving the farm. He drives the tractor by road to Humphrey Head and then I take over once we are on the sands. The three of them – Barry, Mike and John – can sit side by side in comfort whilst I drive over the Bay and out to the River Kent. All this preparation would not come easy these days on my own. Not because I am older – I never think of my age – but because the Bay itself is changing fast and not for the better.

My only access to the sands now with my tractor is to travel by road, through the village of Allithwaite and then take the narrow lane on the left marked to Humphrey Head and the Holy Well. This can take much longer than when it was possible to access the sands from Cart Lane Crossing, which is a stone's throw from Guides Farm, or the alternative one at Kents Bank railway station.

Out on the sands and clear of the marsh after taking over the driving seat, I choose the route as I go along, avoiding gullies and dykes that all run back east towards the river – the lowest part of the Bay. I keep on higher-level sand, which makes it a more comfortable ride for my helpers. It is just impossible to attempt to cross the river in the tractor at any point, so I drive to the part of the Bay that I think looks the most suitable, bring the tractor to a halt close to the river and then look and study the next move.

I check that the sand across the tractor wheel is firm before we prepare to cross the River Kent barefooted. At this point we are about six miles out into the Bay and looking at a very wide river. I always write the tide times on the back of my hand before I leave home. If everything is okay, we take off our wellies and roll our trouser legs up. We then gather our ash walking sticks, which we use to test the firmness of the sand, and set off crossing the river slowly – prodding and testing and hoping that its bed is free from quicksand.

If I am satisfied with what we have found, I make back to the tractor and drive through the river to meet my helpers at the other side. They jump aboard the transport box and we drive on across the Bay to White Creek, choosing the route as we go. This is not easy, with large areas of quicksand to be avoided and alternative routes to be sought every time we have a walk. Although safe, these new routes can make the crossing much further in miles, taking us longer than previous years.

Now work has to start on our return journey back across the Bay from White Creek at Arnside and we put the 'brobs' at intervals all the way back to the river. We next have to test the whole bed of the Kent to the width I have chosen for at least 500 walkers to cross safely on the following two days, and then we put in the 'brobs' on both sides of the river as markers.

If the day has gone well, we climb aboard the tractor and transport box and drive well away from the River Kent onto much higher ground and stop for a while. Barry pours the coffee from the flask and we reflect on what we have achieved. I like to ring Olive at this point to let her know that the walks will be going ahead and it is all systems go. She is then able to tell all enquirers the good news.

This can be a really hard day and we have earned our coffee and short break. We then set off to make our way back across the sands feeling good. The track across the marsh at Humphrey Head is not a good one with each high tide scouring out the sand in the deep gullies. They are so steep that John has to put heavy weights on the front of the tractor to prevent the front wheels coming up off the ground. We have to carry shovels and try to improve the track following each high tide and heavy rainfall. Once back on the narrow and bumpy road it can be difficult when meeting up with other vehicles, which we do from time to time. We have to cross the railway near Wraysholme Tower Farm and then continue to the main road junction, the A590, near to Allithwaite village and along clear of the houses.

Once a police car drove past and pulled us up. The policeman was not in a good mood and asked us questions. Where had we been and what had we been doing? He then told us to get off the box and walk. He didn't ask how far we were going but said in an awful manner, 'Just get off that thing and walk.' Luckily we were not too far from home but we were all so tired. I drove on ahead and waited for my three pals at the top of the steep hill at Carter Road. They jumped aboard and we drove the last few hundred yards in style down the hill to Guides Farm. We did not know we were doing wrong, but he did say that we were not allowed to ride in a transport box in that way.

Across the Bay

On the day of the walk, my daughter Jean drives my friend Mike and I to Arnside, which is much more reliable than the train. We meet up with the walkers who are made up of various groups and there are usually about 450 or so waiting for the Guide to arrive. Arnside is such a lovely compact little seaside village with some really good shops and public houses, one named The Albion, but away from the front it has now got built up and spread over quite a large area. It always seems to be busy, whether it be the weekend of the walks or even during the week. I think the Bay walks and myself may have had something to do with this small village now being so popular. I usually ask Jean to drop Mike and I off on the brow of the hill at the old toilets and antique shop. These toilets are now closed but have been replaced by new ones just across the road and down at shore level. These are in great demand on walk days but you have to pay for the pleasure!

The walkers are usually in groups when we arrive and looking forward to be off. Many seem to hang around on the stone jetty, others near to the war memorial in front of The Albion, all waiting for me to arrive. The starting point is further along the promenade outside the grounds of Ash Meadow. It is a much safer place away from the busy traffic.

It is essential for me to travel light across the nine or so miles of the Bay. I carry a haversack with a waterproof, cap and my whistle, a drink and my thumb stick, which I am never without whilst on the sands. I always have the tide times – morning and evening – written down on my hand, which is important. Olive likes me to have eaten before leaving home, but I eat very little prior to my walks and feel better for this.

It is a great sight to see 450 or so walkers all setting out from Ash Meadow, taking the footpath along the edge of the shoreline and then on to the sand, over the rocks and through the caravan park at Newbarns Farm. This is a three-quarter of an hour journey before arriving on the sands at

Prodding and testing the sands has to be done ahead of every walk, as the channels are constantly changing. There is always the danger of quicksand – and the ash walking sticks can suddenly plunge much deeper. (Ian Hughes – 2)

Cedric heads off with a large group of walkers along the shoreline at Arnside. He always feels this is a great sight. (Neil Stanley)

Talking to assembled walkers before heading out into the Bay. Cedric always has his thumb stick and walks bare-footed. (Ian Hughes)

Kents Bank railway station, the finishing point for all the walks. (Neil Stanley)

Dogs in all breeds and sizes are joining the cross-Bay walk in increasing numbers. Most – but not all – love splashing in the water. (Neil Stanley; Ian Hughes)

White Creek where you can then see the vastness of Morecambe Bay. It takes about twenty minutes or so for all the walkers to arrive at this point, so I usually find somewhere to sit on a relatively dry rock and have a drink and wait for everyone to catch up. Then we're off!

Mike and I always go barefooted – this is the Flookburgh fishermen's tradition that I have always maintained since leaving school and following the sands. The distance across the Bay can vary so much according to the changes and where we are able to cross the river. The 2012 season involved a much longer route and was taking us over four hours but all the walks still finish at Kents Bank railway station.

In this modern age of computers, the Morecambe Bay Walks are so widely known, both nationally and internationally, and a much larger number of people want to cross the Bay. Many charities now raise much needed money by participating in the walks. Those taking part get others to sponsor them, so not only do they raise money for their chosen charity, but they also thoroughly enjoy what they are doing. The good thing about the walks is that they accommodate people of all ages, who experience something special in their lives that is never forgotten.

Specific requests are quite common these days. I never thought this would happen – but it does:

- *A husband and wife's special birthday or anniversary treat.*
- *A family reunion with a walk across the Bay.*
- *The scattering of a loved one's ashes.*

Also becoming very popular is for walkers to bring along their dogs, and it is good to see them enjoying their freedom and chasing after one another. They come in all breeds and sizes.

When we eventually reach the River Kent, I organise the party between the markers of laurel, get them to make a wide spread and then ask that all dogs are put on leads for safety reasons. Most dogs love to swim across, but others take a dislike to water and try to leap up onto their owners' laps. When we reach the other side safely the dogs are once again let off their leads and are free to roam. On a walk across the Bay, the larger groups do tend to get spread out at times, but it is not a race and people can take their time. This is when I blow my whistle and stop everyone at the front to allow the slower walkers to catch up.

On one walk a large Alsatian dog suddenly ran towards me, grabbed my stick and wouldn't let it go. It had such a hold and was growling at me as I tried my best to retrieve it. The dog was much stronger than me and more determined, so I had to give in and let go and it ran off with my stick. I did not see the owner of the dog on the sands. But when we set foot on the shore at Kents Bank railway station, this man came over to me carrying my stick, which was bitten to shreds, and apologised for his dog's behaviour. Fortunately my friend Mike makes sticks for a hobby and a few days later he arrived down at Guides Farm with a brand new replacement. I had never thought about taking out an insurance policy for my beloved thumb stick!

3. Unforgettable Crossings

The Chinese Wheelbarrow

Back in 1974 I received a letter with a request for my services as Guide to accompany a man and his Chinese Wheelbarrow, or desert cart, on a walk from one side of the Bay to the other. I wondered what kind of a project it could be, but then a further letter arrived with all the details of the desert cart. It was a lightweight construction with the load carried in long narrow boxes on either side of a 5ft diameter wheel, thus putting the weight on the cart and not on the driver. A sail was used to take advantage of any favourable wind, leaving only the guiding of the cart to the driver and enabling him to cover many more miles than would have been the case had he to push or pull the load on a conventional cart.

The whole idea was to test the cart in the stringent conditions of the Bay before taking it out to the Sahara desert for further tests, after which it was hoped to put it into production. It would have been of great use to people in such an area, who could not afford motorised transport or camel to move their wares. The design was based on the Chinese sailing wheelbarrow. A barrow or cart such as this had been used for over two thousand years by people of the Orient to carry loads many times their own weight.

The Morecambe Bay test was covered by a BBC 'Nationwide' helicopter. Although things went fairly well out in the Bay, it was apparently a different matter when the cart reached the Sahara. There the fluctuations in wind strength were much greater. At times the wind was so strong that the wheelbarrow had to be held firmly against it and then suddenly it would drop and the barrow would be over on its side.

The wheels were found to be too narrow and all-in-all the going was very difficult. The journey of two thousand miles took three months. Eventually, it was decided not to put the cart into production but the prototype is preserved in store at the Science Museum in South Kensington. This was one of the more unusual trips I made across Morecambe Bay.

Geese across the Bay

Something different to anything I had done previously resulted from a request from Lucy Muller, a Whitby farmer. She wanted to raise money for an arthritis sufferer and wondered if it would be

A gaggle of geese are successfully led across the Bay in July 2000. Cedric is accompanied by his granddaughters Danielle Nickson (right) and Amy Robinson, with Lucy Miller driving the geese at the rear. (Paul Nickson)

possible for me to take twenty-seven geese across the Bay.

The starting place was in the grounds of Furness Abbey on the west coast, where they put up for the night and then set out on their long trek to Whitby on the east coast. I agreed to take them, but had no idea how they would behave in such an open space as Morecambe Bay. After leaving the marsh behind at Kents Bank and moving out onto the sands, the geese followed me wherever I went. I was just amazed at them!

Crossing the River Kent was a wonderful sight, as there was quite a strong flow that they had to battle against to keep together, but they did. After this successful crossing, they followed me in a line as we made for White Creek, where Lucy met up with some of her helpers. Here they put up for the night in order to be fresh for an early start the next morning. I've no doubt that the crossing of the sands of Morecambe Bay was a success and probably the highlight of their long trek back to Whitby.

Cedric on the sands with his dedicated helper Mike Carter. They much prefer barefoot walking, but it can cause problems with sore feet as happened with Mike's brother Terry during preparations for the cross-Bay run. (Terry Marsh)

The Sandpiper trailer can be invaluable, although it has unkindly been described as providing 'an exciting but very rickety ride that is not for the faint-hearted'! (Ian Hughes)

Open to all traffic?

Going back now to 1991, this was a time when Lancashire County Council submitted an Order to the Secretary of State for the Environment for confirmation. The object was to modify the Definitive Map and Statement for the area of Morecambe Bay, reclassifying roads used as public footpaths as byways open to all vehicular traffic.

Slyne with Hest Bank Parish Council objected to the draft Order in the strongest possible terms, as did four individuals. Lancaster City Council and South Lakeland District Council, along with Grange over Sands Town Council, supported the reclassification. The first Order was made on 14th July 1992. Such concerns as suitability, safety and the environmental impact of vehicular use had been uppermost in the minds of objectors and those consulted, but the County Council – whilst not underestimating their importance – considered that they were not relevant.

Unusually, most of the route is subject to tides, shifting river patterns and the instability of the sands. After substantial investigations and consultation, it was concluded that there was little or no evidence of current or recent use by those crossing the sands by whatever means. I supported this view in my official capacity as Queen's Guide to the Sands. However, the historical evidence provided by cartographers, writers and from other records confirmed that over prolonged periods a well-defined route had been used by horse-drawn vehicular traffic.

The alignment of the route, as well as the existence of rights of way, had been widely challenged. So too had the legal principle whereby users can depart from the defined route because it is often impassable. Yet, however physically it was ill defined, the Secretary of State was invited to reclassify the route across the sands of Morecambe Bay as a byway open to all traffic. This is how it now stands, but not without incidents. Almost immediately after this was made public, enquiries were never ending. Some had the idea that it was a hard surface road across the Bay. Lots of these people soon had second thoughts when I explained to them about the crossing. On more than one occasion John and I were waiting down at the railway station crossing for the all clear to proceed, when two 4 x 4 vehicles pulled up behind our tractor. We asked them what they were about to do and they said they were going to drive across the Bay to Hest Bank. They produced the Ordnance Survey map, thinking that if they followed the line shown, it would be easy going! They got quite a shock when we explained the situation and what they would encounter, so they very soon decided to abandon the idea.

One family did take it into their heads to set out from Bolton-le-Sands with their almost brand new 4 x 4 to cross the Bay to Grange. They got the vehicle stuck fast in the sands just 200 yards from the shore. They were reluctant to leave it, but unknown to them the tide was on the turn. Luckily, someone from the shore saw the incident happen and informed the Coastguard. Their thoughts were for the family and getting them safely to the shore. They are not there to retrieve vehicles but in this case they were able to rescue the car and the family who were really grateful.

Not very long after that incident, a second attempt was made by a family to cross in a 4 x 4 and they came to grief in almost the same place. The car is still there with just the roof showing as a reminder of how dangerous these sands can be. Had it been much further out into the Bay it would probably have been completely washed away with the force of the tides.

Yes, I agree that this is the most risky byway in the whole of Britain. The enquiries from 4 x 4 owners have got fewer and fewer since these incidents, but I have offered my services to Land Rover enthusiasts and safely taken them across the Bay and back again.

A Great Run

Early in August 2010 I had an enquiry to see if it would be possible to organise a run across Morecambe Bay with 150 runners taking part. I agreed a date for two of the organisers to come to Guides Farm and we would talk it through. They were James Thurlow and Bruce, the events director, who were both runners and looked very athletic standing about six feet tall. The date they had in mind was Friday, 27th August – weather permitting. As it happened, the tides would be right for the day but it would mean setting off at 7.45am. They said that this would not be a problem and that they could get all the runners over to the other side of the Bay for the early start.

I decided that the race should start from the foreshore out from Bolton-le-Sands. Access from the village was to follow St Michael's Lane, which takes traffic over a railway crossing, past a few houses on either side of the road and down onto a hard surfaced road that leads to a farm and café with ample parking. High water times that day were 1.10am and 1.30pm.

I reckoned that for safety reasons we needed to be clear of the River Kent by 10.30am, which was three hours before high water, dependent on the weather on the day – strong winds and the like. It took me, Barry, John and Mike three days to mark out the route with laurel branches. The first day we went from Bolton-le-Sands out to the River Keer, which runs into the Bay from Carnforth and a bit beyond. It was not an easy task, as we had to carry the laurels and the heavy crowbar, which we put well down into the sands to make way for the markers. This was so they would stay put for at least a few days and serve their purpose because the runners needed a definite and clear route to follow.

The next day Barry and John were away, so Mike and his brother Terry and I walked quite a long way out from Silverdale. We got as far as Jenny Brown's Point to meet up with the 'brobs' we had put in the day previously – marking the way as we went along. As I always walk bare-footed on the sands and Mike does the same, Terry thought he would follow suit. But with not being used to walking in this way, his feet soon became sore and we had to keep waiting for him to catch us up. It was quite a while before his feet got back to normal and he said that he never ever wanted to walk barefooted on those sands again!

On the Thursday we decided to take the tractor and the Sandpiper trailer to the sands. Our route was through Allithwaite and once clear of the village, where the road narrows, we were to take a left turn from the main road into the lane signposted 'Humphrey Head and Holy Well'. Once again

Over: A 'most wonderful event' occurred in August 2010 when some 150 runners crossed the Bay. These scenes show them assembling for the 'off', heading out into the Bay, running down a side channel, and finally plunging into the water. (James Kirby - 4)

Mike was absent and his brother Terry came along to help.

Just before turning off the main road, we had a blow out in one of the Sandpiper wheels but managed to continue so as to be clear of the traffic. Luckily there was a wide grass verge where we were able to unhitch the tractor from the trailer and then think what to do next – as time was of the essence. We had lots of laurel bushes and a heavy crowbar on board, which took up a lot of room and left little space even for one passenger. John and I suggested that the two of us would go ahead with the tractor as planned, because we really needed to run the route and mark out the river and the Grange over Sands side with the remaining laurels. We clambered aboard and set out on our journey via Humphrey Head, leaving Terry behind with his mobile phone to ring Raymond, my son-in-law, who would come with the right tools and a spare wheel – which thankfully he did!

We two headed out across the Bay towards Silverdale, crossing the River Kent, which was split in two and running between knee and thigh deep. Then on in a line for Jenny Brown's Point to cross at a 'lyrin' – the term used by the older fishermen for areas that are no longer the main river channel. They still hold a lot of water but there is very little flow. About 300 to 400 yards down from this 'lyrin' are stones, which re-appeared with the dramatic changes in the Bay that brought them to light after being buried under the sand for over a hundred years. These stones extended straight out from the village of Silverdale. I was now more than pleased with the route and, although the River Kent was very wide, it was good for the runners.

On 27th August a most wonderful event began on a lovely early morning. Mike travelled round to Bolton-le-Sands to make sure the runners got off to a good start and to check our markers were still in place. He carried a mobile phone and he kept us informed of what was happening. The runners did well and made good time. Some were in the Silverdale area within half an hour after setting off, although many were a long way back.

I asked John to take me out to meet the runners. We now had the Sandpiper trailer, and when I was satisfied that they were all managing well I suggested to John that he take me back to the river and drop me off. From here I watched the runners as they passed me – all giving me a wave as they crossed the River Kent. John made back across the sands to keep an eye on any stragglers, but we also had someone on a quad bike doing the same thing. Eventually all runners were clear from the river and up onto safe higher ground, some heading for Humphrey Head and others for Cark Airfield. The early runners made for Cowprom Point.

My responsibility was over at Humphrey Head – and my team and I were very pleased that the event had gone off so smoothly and safely. Barry missed the race but I am sure he would have liked to have been with us on the day, as he just loves being out on these sands and is certainly a great help to me.

Quite an experience!

I well remember one organised drive with Land Rovers. None of the enthusiasts ever reckoned that this was going to be an easy task. This story had begun a couple of months earlier when they were driving on rocky lanes up in the fells of the Lake District. Clearly marked on the Ordnance Survey maps were two lines of the most intriguing byways they had ever seen – because they went out to sea!

Both led into Morecambe Bay from the Cartmel peninsula of south Cumbria. The shortest of them headed west across the estuary of the River Leven to the town of Ulverston. But the more interesting, and the longer by some margin, headed east from Kents Bank before making the marathon crossing to the Lancashire coast a little to the north of Morecambe.

It was agreed between them that without local knowledge it would be very dangerous. One of them lived pretty close to the Bay. A few years back some friends had attempted driving across and nearly lost a Range Rover in quicksand. He himself had walked across the Bay with me previously and said that he would never ever attempt it in a Land Rover without a Guide. I was the only man who could get them across safely, but they were doubtful that I would agree to help. Morecambe Bay is after all a haven of wildlife, although the birds don't seem to mind some disturbance. As I travel across these sands so often, I think they can recognise my old tractor and stay put on their feeding grounds.

Eventually a date was set for this adventure. It could not take place at a weekend because of the walks across the Bay, which had been organised months in advance, so these vehicles had to be taken across during the week with much higher tides. Familiarity with this terrain never breeds contempt, as the rivers, dykes, sands and gullies change with every tide. Along with my helpers, I had therefore spent the previous day planning a safe route and marking it with laurel branches.

It was reckoned a convoy of three Land Rovers would be about right, as if one of them got stuck the other two would be able to pull him out. After spending the previous day sussing out the area and watching those menacing tides advancing and receding across the estuary, the moment had arrived for the drivers to meet up with me and my son Paul by the sea wall at Kents Bank railway station. They arrived on time, eager with anticipation. There isn't much chance to hang around on these trips to take photographs, so they attached a remote controlled camera to the roof of one of the Defenders with tape.

I am always strict to time when organising such events, so we quickly got the convoy moving through the crossing gates, down the railway embankments and out onto the salt marsh. The tides were still in the droppings – meaning they were getting lower in height and the sheep were grazing on the salt marsh. The weather on the day was balmy. One minute we had the warm sunshine of summer, then we were almost blown off course with stormy winds and driving rain, and at this stage we had barely left the safety of the shore. I was in the lead car, which was open-topped, pointing out the route, as my markers couldn't be seen until we were almost on them. Eventually we reached the River Kent, at least 150 yards wide, and to the drivers of these three vehicles it must have looked menacing.

I brought the convoy to a halt, stepped down and gave a quick word of advice to the drivers. The first vehicle in line was a nineteen-year-old S111 with a 2.25 litre petrol engine. By all accounts the engine had been kicking and sputtering all the way to Kents Bank, and when it came to driving across the River Kent they simply disconnected the fan to prevent water being thrown all over the electrics.

We were then ready for the off. As they drove into the river it was difficult to keep on a straight course because of the strong current. It seemed to take all their might to hold the steering wheel firm, as the ebbing tide appeared to be taking them down river. This is normal for anyone who has never crossed a fast-moving river like the Kent during higher tides and the drivers definitely thought they were floating.

At such times I always advise not to look down at the moving water, but stare straight ahead to the other side and everything will be alright. They all looked very nervous through the river, but once out on the far side we were soon speeding across the smooth wet sand, spray flying from the wheels as we drove on towards White Creek with the wind and weather behind us. As we drew to a halt, they all jumped down from their vehicles to celebrate. We had travelled about seven miles across the Bay – four as the crow flies. The rain did let up for this brief stop and the sun shone down on us as we lined up for our photo shoot.

Soon it was time to return. Although the rain had eased, the wind had increased to gale force and brought in the tide much earlier than would happen on a calm day. It was so windy that the higher sandbanks were drying out and creating a sandstorm. The River Kent, which had seemed daunting on the way over, now looked positively dangerous. It was at least 200 yards wide with big 'white horses' – a fisherman's term for the white-topped waves in these conditions. I was concerned and the drivers looked terrified. The fan on the petrol-engined Land Rover should have been unbolted again, but the horrible weather meant that water and sand had got into the electrics. The engine wouldn't switch off, so the fan could not be removed. We had to keep moving – and halfway across the engine started missing badly, running on just two cylinders.

It was a miracle that this vehicle reached the other side. I was not happy, thinking that we might have to abandon it in midstream and us passengers would have to jump out into waist-deep water. Fortunately the vehicle managed to limp over and away from the river and eventually we arrived safe and sound at the Kents Bank shore. Quite an experience – but just one of many!

Wheelchairs on the sands

After being given an honorary degree at Lancaster University of Science and Technology in 1999, I agreed to organise a cross-Bay walk for them to raise money for disabled students. They asked me if it would be alright to include six students in wheelchairs. I had to give this a lot of thought, as such a venture had not previously been attempted. Eventually I suggested to them that if they were keen for this to happen, I would go along with their ideas, but this must be well organised beforehand as there would be no turning back once we got well out into the Bay.

My suggestion to them was to organise four big strong lads to each wheelchair, two pushing and the other two pulling with ropes. These lads, however strong, would eventually get tired, so a backup must be there ready to give them a break. On the day of the walk – a fine day – everything went off smoothly until we came to the River Kent.

As we entered the river and the water deepened, the lads in charge of the wheelchairs thought that if they pressed down on the handles, the disabled students' legs would be raised high and dry from the water. This did not seem to work because now their midriffs were under water. The look on their faces soon told us that they were enjoying every minute of this one-off experience. They got a wetting but this must have been the highlight of this special crossing of the sands – and they, and I, would remember it for a very long time.

4. Those in Trouble!

As time goes by, memories of the Bay don't fade and I certainly have lots of them from the experiences I have had over many years. Looking back almost thirty years, I remember the day when I was asked by John Duerdon, the Arnside Coastguard, if I would become an auxiliary to assist their team of volunteers.

Arnside Coastguard Station is built on the upper reaches of the Kent estuary and is slightly hidden. The only way that they could look at the vast expanse of the Bay in an emergency was to travel up to the top of Arnside Knott, which gave them panoramic views, and look through binoculars. If an incident happened on the upper reaches of the Bay near to Arnside – and they do quite often with holidaymakers getting stuck in the mud – then they are on hand to do a rescue.

When I joined the Coastguard auxiliary, John Duerdon was in charge of a team of about twelve men – a jolly good team they were who held a lot of respect for their leader. We met occasionally in Arnside in the hall belonging to the sailing club. There was always someone from Liverpool Coastguard Station and Walney at these meetings. Everyone got on really well and it was suggested that I be given a powerful VHF radio if I was to assist with incidents in the Bay. With me having good access, knowledge of the sands and the river channels, they thought I would be of great help if I were needed. From Guides Farm I have such a clear view of the Bay and own an ex

A group of walkers passes Arnside Coastguard Station, built on the upper reaches of the Kent estuary and slightly hidden from view. (Neil Stanley)

⚠ Danger

Beware fast rising tides

Quick sands

Hidden channels

SIRENS WARN OF INCOMING TIDE

IN EMERGENCY PHONE **999**
AND ASK FOR THE COASTGUARD

Signs in Arnside warn of the dangers in Morecambe Bay and make it clear that the Coastguard is the emergency point of contact. (Ian Hughes)

army brass telescope with night vision. This was offered to me by my neighbour, Johnny Wright, before I became the Queen's Guide. I bought it from him all those years ago for a fiver – it was fifty years ago to be exact.

On more than one occasion, John contacted me and asked if I would look out from Kirkhead – from there you have a perfect view of every inch of Morecambe Bay. When asked, I would drive to Kents Bank and then carry my very heavy telescope to view the Bay. This was a great help to John and his crew.

My visits to Arnside during the summer are now mostly at weekends to lead the walks across the Bay to Grange over Sands. On many occasions I do meet up with one or two retired members of the Coastguard, and it is good to see them again and have a chat about old times.

I was taken ill a number of years ago and admitted to hospital. Two of my Coastguard colleagues came along to Guides Farm to see Olive and ask if she needed any help. Our large living room has an open fire and has to be lit every day, as this is our only way of heating the water. Olive was struggling to light it as she could not find any dry wood, so she gave the two men a chicken carcase from the fridge and this did the job. Whenever I come across these two now retired Coastguard men, they always mention the day they helped Olive light the living room fire with a chicken carcase and we have a good laugh about it.

Yachts off course

Incidents didn't always happen in daylight hours. A resident of Kents Bank was looking out across the Bay from her sitting room window on a very wet late afternoon. She thought she saw a large yacht sitting out there in the Bay and reported this to the Coastguard. It appeared to have run aground about two miles from the shore, so John Duerdon asked me if I would look through my telescope to see if this was true.

I readily agreed and was able to locate the yacht. It was such a bad night that I rang my friend Mike and asked if he would come with me. He couldn't make it but his brother Terry offered to come along in his place. We met at the railway station at Kents Bank and the weather was closing in fast with very poor visibility. I had a good idea of where this yacht had run aground. We had to drive in the dark, which wasn't easy because I had no lights on my old tractor. There was just an orange light that sat on top of the cab and kept flashing the whole of the time. We had no windscreen wipers either but off we set into the unknown.

I had travelled over the area many times on low tides, but now the tides were high, bringing changes to all the dykes and gullies. It was a totally different environment to what I had experienced the last time I had driven over the area. It was the most uncomfortable ride on the backboard of my tractor for poor old Terry, but he held tight and didn't grumble. All of a sudden we arrived – right on target. This very large yacht was lying on its side at anchor on a high sand bank.

I jumped from my tractor and with my stick I could just reach the cabin window, on which I gave a few taps. A face first emerged and then this figure of a man opened the cabin door. I explained who I was and why I had come out to see whether they were in difficulty. He said that there were no worries and invited us to climb aboard the yacht. We made some excuse. Never hitch a lift with a stranger we thought. We didn't know who they were and they did look a bit dodgy.

I suggested to him that he would have to wait for the next tide and then sail back the way he had come to find deeper waters before making back across the Bay to Arnside. He said he would be alright, as he had a map of the Bay and the channels, and when the tide came in he would sail for Kents Bank and follow the River Kent all the way up to Arnside. I told him that his map was well out of date and the Kent channel was now no longer near Kents Bank or Grange over Sands. The very next day the yacht was nowhere to be seen. He must have sailed back the way he came and disappeared on the morning tide. He had come from the Isle of Man.

A later incident involving a yacht occurred when Arnside Sailing Club organised a sail down the Bay in high tide for a visit to Glasson Dock, near Lancaster. John Duerdon rang me because he felt quite worried. When they had arrived at Glasson there was a yacht missing, so he asked if I would look out into the Bay to see if I could spot anything with my telescope. He described the yacht as being blue and the occupants were a father and two small children. The tides were at their highest and most dangerous. John asked me if I would go out and find them, ascertain their circumstances and let him know.

On locating them, I realised that they had run aground on the far side of the river, so I could not get to them. I drove my tractor as close as possible to the river, jumped down and, cupping my hands together, yelled as loud as I could. It was ages before a man came out of his small cabin and asked what I was doing. I told him who I was and why I had come out to see if they were okay. I explained that John Duerdon had rung me from Glasson Dock because he was very worried after noticing that a yacht was missing from the fleet.

The next tide was a high ten metres and would race in at a gallop. John was really worried for their safety. He thought the yacht might be taken up the estuary during the night when the crew were fast asleep and then bash against the railway viaduct. That didn't need thinking about. The man's reply was to tell John not to worry about them as they had food and water on board. They would put both anchors down and would be okay.

The morning tide did indeed take the yacht and its occupants up the estuary whilst they were sleeping. The anchors did not hold against the force of the tide and luckily for them their yacht came to rest between Holme Island and Arnside railway viaduct. They should have taken notice of John, who had years of experience of the moods and tides of Morecambe Bay.

John has now sadly passed on but somebody like him will never be forgotten. He was special – a real gentleman.

Carrying a gun?

Guides Farm is at times a mini information centre with calls and enquiries coming in from the Coastguard and the Police as well as film services and the general public.

One incident started when a young German student came over to Lancaster Infirmary – as it was called at that time – to learn the medical profession. She had come away from her friends and family, and when she had some free time from the hospital she took the train from Lancaster to Grange over Sands and went for a walk along the promenade. She had no idea of the dangers of

Hovercraft are an invaluable part of the Morecambe Bay rescue service. They can quickly reach areas that a conventional craft would find impossible. (Paul Nickson)

Morecambe Bay and at that time must have been feeling very depressed. She was seen sobbing her heart out by someone who rang Grange over Sands police station and said that this person was going out into the Bay in quite a state. It was thought she was going to commit suicide by walking into the tide.

The police rang me from Grange and said that two of them would leave the police station and go down onto the promenade to investigate what was happening. They would keep me informed and would I stay near the phone. Minutes later, one of them rang me and said that he was following this person out into the Bay and needed my assistance. I put the phone down, looked out of the front door and saw the policeman running, so I jumped over the wall and crossed the railway tracks. I ran all the way until I met up with the policeman. He was chasing this person at speed but the faster we ran the more we were left behind. We were heading towards the lower part of the Bay with the tide now very close to coming in. I asked the policeman to stop for a while to see what happened.

This was the right thing to do, as the person we were chasing now changed direction and headed out towards Humphrey Head well clear of the incoming tide. The policeman was talking to me the whole time and wondered what he was going to do once we caught up. We managed to get close enough but were still quite a distance away when the policeman suddenly grabbed me by the arm and said, "Stop, he is carrying a gun!" I am used to looking long distances with following the sands and when I took a good look – even though far away – I said to the policeman, "This isn't a man we have been following – it's a woman and I don't think she is carrying a gun."

Opposite: The channels and shoreline of Morecambe Bay are subject to constant change – and relying on old maps can be fatal. This view shows the results of tidal erosion at Whistler's Dyke, out from Kents Bank station. (Paul Nickson)

The very same morning I had seen on the sands, close to Guides Farm, a young woman with a bag over her shoulder. She kept stopping and taking photographs. I told the policeman it was the same woman so he said to give her a shout. I cupped my hands together and explained who I was. I didn't say anything else and she stood still. As we approached she seemed very afraid of us two, especially the uniformed policeman.

He had no sympathy at all and gave her a right telling off. Afterwards, when we arrived back at the shore, the policeman took down all the details as he would have to make a report. I perfectly understood the young woman's feelings and said very little to her, but she did agree to take a photograph of me after the policeman had left. She said she felt much better now she was back on the shore.

Cut off by the tide

Bird watching is an infectious hobby these days with lots of enthusiasts and Morecambe Bay has such a variety of waders that can be seen from the safety of the shore – or with a good pair of binoculars. I know that the sands can on a nice day be inviting to a stranger, but to wander out into the Bay without any knowledge of the tides is foolhardy and asks for trouble. I have such a wide view of the sands from our living room window and there is very little goes on out there without me seeing or being able to assist if my services are needed.

I had set a band of nets out in the Bay, about halfway between Cart Lane and Silverdale. They were there to catch the fluke or flounder and anything else that might get caught up in them. To reach the nets I had to cross a stretch of water – not as deep as the main River Kent but quite wide. Although the river has moved away from it, the tide will still run up this stretch of water.

One blustery day I was looking through my telescope when I saw a man walking out from Grange promenade towards my fishing nets. I kept an eye on him and said to Olive that I hoped he knew what he was doing because the tide was due at the nets in around twenty minutes. He arrived at the nets and walked the full length of them, lifting the mesh from the sand level and then quite a way below. I could see the tidal bore – a white wave moving up the river – and with a strong breeze it was wasting no time. I said to Olive that if he left the nets now and made for the shore he would be alright.

I could not believe what I saw next! He stood and watched as the bore rolled up the river past him. Then, instead of moving away and making for the shore where he would have been safe, he strode off in the other direction down the Bay towards Morecambe. When he turned round, he suddenly realised that he was being cut off by the tide and started to run. He was too late.

Although he was on higher ground between the two waters, the tide was lapping nearer and nearer to him. I immediately dialled 999 to the Liverpool Coastguard and they got in touch with Arnside, who launched their dinghy with a powerful outboard motor and were soon on the scene. I had my powerful VHF radio and could talk to the crew.

I stood outside Guides Farm on the lawn, with a clear view of the Bay. The lifeboat crew asked me on which line had I seen the man. I told them that it had been on a line from Guides Farm to the church at Silverdale, but now the tide was choppy and you couldn't see anything. They said that they would sail back and look around the viaduct in the Arnside area – thinking that the big tide might have taken the man up the Bay. They were away for a while, but on their return they headed towards the shore at Cart Lane and said to me over the radio, "Cedric, we are going to sail on the line where you said you first saw him. We will regularly switch off the engine and shout." At the third time of stopping and shouting, I could hear on my radio a faint voice crying for help.

The crew called me and said, "We've got him!" Then I heard them saying that they would make for Grange promenade near to the railway station and have an ambulance waiting to take him to Kendal Hospital, now called Westmorland General. He suffered hypothermia – but he was very lucky to have been between two fast moving tides in a backwater, which held him there. The way he was dressed certainly helped to save his life and keep him afloat. He was also known to have been a strong swimmer, although this would not in any way have helped him. He recovered completely, but I bet he will think twice about walking out into Morecambe Bay without someone with knowledge of its tides and moods.

Two missing children

There can be nothing more exciting than a visit to the seaside when we have the weather to go with it. That is what a couple with two children, a boy and a girl, thought when they chose to holiday at the Lakeland Leisure Caravan Park at Flookburgh.

They had their own car and thought they would go out for the day. Humphrey Head is only a short distance away from where they were staying, so they decided to take a picnic, park the car close to the rocks, assemble their deck chairs and sit down and relax. Their two children would amuse themselves by playing on the sands. On very low tides and fine weather the sands dry out for mile upon mile and it was quite safe for them. Other families had the same idea and there were several cars parked in a row, facing out into the Bay.

I had a phone call from the police headquarters at Penrith saying that this was urgent. Two children had gone missing from Humphrey Head whilst their parents were having a nap and they couldn't find them. They began to think that their children had wandered into the Bay and been drowned with the incoming tide.

I drove down to Humphrey Head as fast as I could and saw several policemen talking on their mobiles. I approached one of them and explained about the phone call from Penrith police station telling me of the situation. I asked if I could talk to the parents, who were really distraught. Their car had been moved about two hundred yards and was stuck in the sands. I said to them, "Can you remember where you saw them last before you fell asleep?" The husband pointed in a south-westerly direction.

Looking across the vast Bay from that point at Humphrey Head in a heat wave, any lay person would have thought it was the tide away in the distance. But what they were seeing was a mirage. I calmed them down when I explained that if the children had walked out into the Bay in that direction, the sands were dry for miles upon end. There had been no tide for four days and it would be another day or two before the tides started to rise and cover the sands. After explaining this to the parents they were feeling a lot better, but they were still concerned that the children were still

The sands off Humphrey Head can often dry out for mile upon mile during fine weather and low tides. (Paul Nickson)

missing.

I have good eyesight and am used to looking long distances across the Bay. I studied the horizon, soon spotting something miles away and hoping that this was the children. The police had some binoculars with them. They thought one person could be seen, but were adamant that in no way could they go out there with their vehicles. One policeman got quite a shock when I said to him, "No, you can't but if I jump in alongside you then we can."

Well, he could not believe what happened next! I kept him going, talking to him and issuing instructions – go right, go left now – avoiding the dykes and keeping him to the hard sand. Once clear of the gullies and dykes we started to travel over the firm sand at speed.

At least four miles out from the shore we pulled alongside one of the youngsters. It was the boy and we then wondered about his sister. He told us that with it being such a hot day they had decided to walk out into the Bay as it looked like a desert. They had had a row and she had walked off making for Flookburgh and the caravan park where they were staying. The policeman phoned the other police at Humphrey Head and told them that we had got the boy safely in the car, but the girl was still missing. They drove through to Flookburgh and eventually came across the young girl and brought her back to her parents. Their car was still stuck fast in the sand, so I organised the Flookburgh fishermen to retrieve the vehicle with their tractors. As the saying goes ,"All's well that ends well!"

5. Filming
– and the famous

Some rescues have been so dramatic that they have attracted the attention of film and TV companies wanting to stage reconstructions. This has particularly been the case with those involving the notorious Morecambe Bay quicksand. Each year my colleagues and friends at the Arnside Coastguard Service carry out at least thirty quicksand rescues, mostly of holidaymakers who walk out and then become trapped. Quicksand is a suspension of sand and water and has very peculiar behaviour. It freezes into a solid mass if you try to move and does not easily let go. If you try to pull out a limb from the quicksand, you have to work against a vacuum left behind, which is almost impossible, especially if you are out there alone.

This is exactly what happened in 1996 to Terry Howlett, a 29-year old, who had left his home in Darlington for a night out in Carnforth. He used to visit the area when on leave from the Navy and thought Morecambe Bay would be the same as it was then. He decided to walk out to Cote Stones beach at Warton, but as he was crossing a gully he realised he was in trouble because his feet were sinking. The more he struggled the deeper he went down up to his waist. Eventually he gave in and the sand around him set like concrete. He was quite a way out from the shore and his cries for help were not heard owing to the driving rain and the direction of the wind.

Cedric is constantly out in the Bay with film crews. Here he is seen with daughter Jean demonstrating the traditional method of cockle fishing. (Paul Nickson)

How he survived the night was a miracle, but luckily for him his shouts were heard the next morning by a Mr Gardner who was looking after his sheep on the marsh. He called the police before seeking reinforcements. Fire, police and paramedics arrived along with the Arnside Coastguards, but time was running out as the tide was well on its way in. By the time Terry was pulled clear the water was up to his neck and rising fast with some of the rescuers actually working below the surface. He was immediately airlifted by a RAF helicopter to the Royal Lancaster Infirmary, suffering from hypothermia. Terry was immensely grateful to the rescue teams who really did save his life. Another ten minutes and he would have drowned!

A reconstruction of this incident was shown on the BBC TV '999' programme. The filming was done close to Morecambe Lodge farm but a stuntman was used as they could not persuade Terry to repeat the performance. I was invited along as technical advisor and Terry was by my side.

Really dangerous

During my lifetime I have been involved in the filming of Morecambe Bay quicksand on several other occasions. The first was with Professor Magnus Pike for a programme called 'Don't Ask Me', with someone asking the question, 'What makes quicksand?' We filmed close to the shore, near Guides Farm, and it was really dangerous. An air sea rescue helicopter was on standby for this filming.

A second filming of quicksand involved an American TV company coming all that way to Morecambe Bay, but they didn't have a stuntman. I had been on the sands and out to the river. This was quite a number of years ago when we had much better weather, so the most dangerous quicksand was always to be found in the river itself, on or close to the edges, and a long way out from the shore.

On the day when the filming was to take place, the producer was not happy to go all that way out into the Bay and said to me, "Can't you find something near to the shore?" Which I did because we had thirty young children with us waiting to be filmed and I had to look after them. I chose the place and as we approached I stopped everyone and drew a line in the soft sand with my stick. I told them that no one had to cross that line because quicksand was really dangerous.

The camera was set up and started to roll and I had to ask one child to volunteer. He had to hold my hand and walk across swiftly as the sand quaked underneath us. As long as we moved fast and did not stop, we would be okay. Although a frightening experience, we made it safely and the film crew were very satisfied.

When I had asked the children for one volunteer they had all put up their hands and it goes to show that youngsters don't see danger. They certainly learned something that no doubt would be a topic of conversation once back in school the following day. Without taking too many risks, this was educational to all the children I took out onto the sands to be filmed for the National Geographic Documentary Programme.

Doing it the German way

The most recent filming involved a German TV company with a famous stuntman who in his nineteen-year career had been a double for Brad Pitt and was eager to be filmed in a quicksand rescue on Morecambe Bay. After receiving their call from Germany, I was to find a suitable area for this to happen. No problem, as Morecambe Bay has the most dangerous quicksand in the whole world. They originally told me that in no way did they need the back up of our local Coastguard, but I did insist that without them on standby in case of emergency this filming could not go ahead. The Coastguard at Liverpool was informed and said they were not happy with the situation. They contacted Arnside Coastguard, Bay Rescue at Flookburgh, the local police and Lancaster and Morecambe Town Councils who were all against the idea. But by this time the Germans had booked their flights to Manchester Airport and their hotels and it was too late to cancel. They were determined to come and film the quicksand rescue.

Liverpool Coastguard rang again to ask me for their e-mail address so that they could contact them and try to put them off, but to no avail, so something had to be worked out rather quickly. I had to describe to the Coastguard where this was about to take place, and also the times of the tide, outgoing and incoming, at the area I had chosen. Still not happy, the Coastguard told me that if the stuntman got into a difficult situation I was to ring 999 no later than low water. This would give the crew at Morecambe Hovercraft Station ample time to travel up the Bay and rescue the man from the quicksand. That never happened.

The plan was to take the crew and the stuntman out to the area chosen from Kents Bank station on the Sandpiper trailer. John, my helper, had put wooden planks to stand on the quicksand if a rescue was needed and had also provided ropes and first aid.

As John drove the tractor towards the station crossing, I was following in my car and in my mirror I saw a Coastguard vehicle close behind. We pulled up at the station and I went to greet the two men from Arnside Coastguard. I had not met them before, although I have been a phone contact in 'Coastguard for Safety on the Sands' for almost thirty years. They asked the whereabouts of the quicksand stunt, which I explained to them as we walked out across the marsh to the area I had marked out the previous day.

There is quicksand and quicksand. The upper reaches of the Bay tend to be a muddy substance, which is still dangerous if you are unlucky to get into it. Deep gullies can have the same effect, but further down the estuary the quicksand can be very scary and vary so much in depth. Arnside Station Officer Nigel Capstick viewed the situation at Kents Bank and said to me, "Cedric, there is no way we can let this filming go ahead, because there is no back up."

Over: Film crews have long been attracted to Morecambe Bay by its spectacular sunrises and sunsets. The first of these two striking photographs shows the whole of the Bay tinted pink during a winter sunrise. In the second view the waters reflect the last rays of an orange sun about to dip below the horizon. (Paul Nickson – 2)

He rang on his mobile to Flookburgh Bay Rescue, who were also not in favour of what was proposed. He then told me that the following day he could muster a rescue team with colleagues from Arnside Coastguard Station. It was suggested first to me and then to the Germans that it was too dangerous to attempt this filming without the full rescue team alongside. Although they seemed very disappointed, they listened to the alternative suggestion he put to them and they agreed.

Filming in a much safer environment at Sandside the following day went according to plan. I watched patiently as the cold north-westerly wind penetrated my clothing and was asked now and again to walk alongside the stuntman. He spoke to me first in German, then in English, and I explained to him what he should do when he was about to go down in the quicksand. I had a microphone attached to my jumper.

This is how the situation was solved and not in the way it was portrayed in a local paper. I know – I was there! As we parted company I was told that the filming was being done for the German TV show 'Galilo'.

Memorable moments

Apart from its quicksand, Morecambe Bay has always been of interest in many other ways to film crews and journalists. With 120 square miles of sea, sand, rivers and gullies – not forgetting the most outstanding sunrises and sunsets ever to be seen – is there any wonder that they find the Bay a haven for their work? It has become known nationally and internationally and always with good feedback. The list of film crews and celebrities seems endless over the years – and they still come.

There was a huge gathering on 30th May 1985 when a truly historic event took place. It was the first attempt in over one hundred years when I guided horse-drawn carriages across the Bay. The Duke of Edinburgh was in the leading carriage and I was sitting alongside him. It was not the usual crossing owing to the dramatic changes in the Bay, but this drive was organised to start from Silverdale and finish at Kents Bank, a distance of about four miles. This event stands out in my memory as the most wonderful and special of all time.

There seems to have been so many other special occasions when looking back over my years as Queen's Guide. Many well-known people have carried out the walk. They include historian AJP Taylor, who was so nervous out on the Bay when we crossed over an area of soft sand that I offered him a piggyback. He took up my offer!

Others have included TV personality Bob Langley, holiday presenter Judith Chalmers, 'Blue Peter' presenter Simon Groom (accompanied by 'Blue Peter' dog Goldie), TV presenter Matthew Kelly, Melvyn Bragg, American author Bill Bryson, comedian and writer Victoria Wood, and the one and only Hayley Cropper (Julie Hesmondhalgh) from 'Coronation Street'.

We recently had a surprise visit from Peter Carr, who about forty years ago made a short film for BBC TV that they called 'The Sandman'. He and his partner had been holidaying in the Lake District and decided to call once again at Guides Farm. They immediately recognised us both but we could not say the same about him.

In 1980, Border TV arranged for me to be filmed with Sir Harry Secombe for a programme called 'Highway'. The same year Alistair McDonald accompanied me across the Bay from Hest Bank and the walk was filmed from beginning to end. Later that year I was once again out on the sands being filmed with David Bellamy for a children's programme called 'Bellamy's Bugle'. Then along came Russell Harty and on the day of filming the weather was awful, but we seemed to manage to carry on.

'Treasure Hunt' was wonderful to watch on TV and on this day, out there in the Bay, I was wondering if the helicopter and crew were ever going to find us, but eventually they did. Paul Heiney from the TV programme 'Countryfile' has been to Guides Farm on two occasions, with both visits covering the dangerous areas of quicksand. In 2003 I was filmed, once again, with Alan Titchmarsh.

Rick Stein, the well-known seafood chef, went out into the Bay for some cockles and flounder from my fishing nets. Back at Guides Farm we cooked the fish and had a banquet. After tasting the flounders he said they were special and equally as good as fresh halibut. One of the memories I have of this trip out in the Bay is that Rick, when being filmed, couldn't remember his lines and the cameraman had to retake it several times.

Neil Oliver was the presenter of the TV series 'Coast', and I featured in one of these popular programmes that has been repeated many times. I enjoyed his company and it was a pleasure to film with him. Ian McKellen chose Morecambe Bay as the perfect setting for a film he was to make. My job was to take the film crew out to a location where it was safe and let them get on with it. This was most interesting to me as I just sat quietly and watched.

I was really surprised by my next visitor, who was Michael Portillo for the TV programme 'Great British Railway Journeys'. I met him at the garden gate of Guides Farm and, although the cameras had already been set up, I had no idea at all whom I was going to greet. As soon as he shook my hand, I looked at him and said, "I think I have seen you somewhere before – probably on TV." I was not thinking that he had been in the Conservative government and he started laughing. We then had to take the shots again!

Olive is a very quietly spoken person, but when told that we were to be filmed for the 'Flog It' TV programme we were both quite excited. We were both on camera inside the living room at Guides Farm and I was filmed out in the Bay. This programme was a success and there are more to follow.

So many things seem to have happened here at Guides Farm. They range from endless enquiries for information about the guided walks through to the writing of my books. All of these have been different but all about life and times on Morecambe Bay.

My first attempt to write was published in hardback in 1980 and called *Sand Pilot of Morecambe Bay*. In 1984 I wrote *One Man's Morecambe Bay*. In 1989 *Sandman of Morecambe Bay* was published and a reprint of my first book came out in 1998 as a paperback. *Sand Walker* was published in 2000 with *40 Years on Morecambe Bay* in 2003 and *Between the Tides* in 2007. Following this was *Sandman* in 2009 and now once again I have put pen to paper. I am hoping that this latest book will be as popular as my previous titles!

The Duke of Edinburgh, seated next to Cedric Robinson, during the historic carriage crossing in May 1985. (Tom Stephen)

Melvyn Bragg and Cedric setting out across the Bay from Hest Bank in May 1985. (Leslie Stringer)

6. Farming and Fishing

I so often reflect on our move to Guides Farm and how it gave us lots of opportunities in those earlier years. I applied to the Trustees for permission to cultivate part of the land and grow our own vegetables. I already had my Ferguson tractor and equipment, which I used when I lived in Flookburgh before getting married to Olive. My parents had a stall on the outside market at Barrow in Furness and we had two smallholdings that kept us quite busy. I was also following the sands for cockles, shrimps and flukes, which sold very well in Barrow.

Guides Farm, solidly built to resist the weather, has a big open fire in the sitting room. (Peter Cherry; Paul Nickson)

Here at the farm we put out a small sign to get some customers, but in fact the vegetables were of such good quality that they sold themselves. Early potatoes were planted in March and always did well. Carrots were the same. I usually dug up the potatoes and bunched the carrots for Olive to sell when I was out on the sands. She frequently had to go round the back field to dig up potatoes for customers when I was not available to do this for her.

We needed some stock to keep the land in order and the two of us would follow the farm sales and purchase young calves. They were bred much smaller all those years ago. You could put a calf into a large hessian sack and tie some string round the top with just its head sticking out – and it took no harm. Today the breeds are much bigger and heavier and no way would you put them in a sack – you need a proper cattle trailer.

We also purchased four donkeys and two small Shetland ponies, which we had for many a year. Eventually when the time came to part with them, they all went to very good homes.

With my parents following the market, we thought it would be a good thing if we could rear some turkeys to sell at Christmas. I purchased two good hen huts from a pal of mine from the next village – Allithwaite. They were sectional, so there was a bit of work involved in taking them down, transporting them to Guides Farm and then erecting them up in the paddock. We had plenty of room with the two huts and decided to buy in twenty young turkeys at six months old. They were white and were an enormous breed. I would fasten them in at night on account of foxes in the area.

Once I was late back from the sands and went up to see if all the turkeys had gone in for the night. I closed the door thinking this was the case, but as I walked down towards the gateway to the first field I could see that several had perched up in the large ash tree. I thought they would be alright and that they would be down in the morning when I went out with their feed.

Next morning I got such a shock. Those almost fully grown turkeys were strewn across the meadow – all dead! A fox had killed all of them. I am not a shooting man, but this annoyed me so much that our son Robert offered to go up to the paddock with me the very next morning before daybreak and take his shotgun. We sat and waited and then we heard this peculiar noise – barking but different to that of a dog. This was the fox, which had probably come back to carry away one of the turkeys he had previously killed. We saw him when it came light but at a distance. He lived to kill again but not at Guides Farm. Henceforth we were always on the ball and fastened all our poultry away at night so that we knew they would be safe.

All these years on, I still keep about thirty hens of mixed breeds – Wellsomers, Black Rock and Hybrids. Two years ago I was at my local farm food suppliers in Kendal and asked if they knew of anyone who had any pullets for sale. They said I was lucky because a lady had just been in from Ireleth, near Askam, and she was desperate to give away some pullets to a good home. They gave me her telephone number and I rang her as soon as I got home. She described where she lived and we agreed a time to go there the very next day. She had these pullets fastened up in a small wooden hut, surrounded by low fencing to make quite a large pen. This was behind the house and on the side of the fell, on rough ground. She said she didn't want any money for the pullets, just as long as they were going to a good home.

She was so upset as a fox had got quite a number of these young pullets and they had just started to lay. She explained that she and her husband had heard such a commotion out the back and both they and their Labrador dog had rushed out of the house towards the hen run. The fox was inside the run, chasing the hens everywhere. Outside the pen a rather larger dog fox sat watching them – and this was in broad daylight. They scared the fox away, but it would be back again to do more damage. When I looked at the pen I saw that the wire wasn't high enough and enabled the foxes to come and go as they pleased.

The pullets were really forward in condition and there was no way that I wanted to take them away without giving her some kind of payment in return. She said again, "As long as they are going to a good home I don't mind. But can my husband come and see if they have settled down?" I agreed, but as far as I know he never did turn up at the farm. That was almost two years ago and I have still got them. They have been – and still are – very good layers, so quiet and contented and following me around.

Nowadays there are urban foxes around that have been caught and brought out into the country, but they cannot fend for themselves. They are just let loose but they haven't had the same upbringing as the foxes out in the wild. Last summer, I had just come back from doing some shopping in Grange and was parking my car when I heard my hens making such a noise. I rushed round to the pen and saw feathers everywhere. All the hens looked very unsettled and some had perched up one of our apple trees.

One of my Welsomer hens had been grabbed by the fox. All its feathers from the rear end were missing, with injuries on its back and on one of its legs. I put it in a small box in the large hut and fed it with corn and fresh water each day. It couldn't walk. After a while, when it seemed a little better, I opened the box but left it in the hut. The hen didn't get any exercise this way so eventually I let it out among the others. It is now two years on and, although I have to lift it out of the hut every day, it is fine once down in the hen run. It can manage to go back in at night and fly onto the perch.

It was almost a miracle, because following this incident I met up with a famous fell runner, Josh Taylor, who is a Lake District farmer. When I told him of this hen, he said, "It will never do any good, Cedric, you may just as well wring its neck." He said that once hens have been got by a fox and have been injured, they get gangrene in the wound and can never survive. Yet we still have that same hen today and she is as good as new.

Horses and ponies

I suppose I am soft natured, but I have a love of all animals. Horses and ponies are my favourites – I am mad about them. We have had many over the years, but I will always remember a Fell pony we had called Chester. One of the best, he was of show standard and had everything the breed possessed. We bought him as a four year old. He was hardy and lived outside, summer and winter.

My cousin Jennifer and her husband Maurice, who live in Ulverston, came to see him one day and suggested that he would make a first class driving pony. Jennifer was very knowledgeable and well into ponies and carriage driving in shows. She had taken so many awards and knew what she was talking about. She suggested that she and Maurice would come through and bring one of her traps that would suit Chester – I already had plenty of harness. On the day Chester went really well and did not put a foot wrong. I climbed up into the driving seat with the reins, with Jennifer and Maurice either side of his head, which had leading reins attached. We were all so pleased with him as we travelled along Cart Lane, then up and down Carter Road.

Cedric is not normally associated with a bow tie and a topper, but here he is in proper regalia with his cob Charlie. The venue is the 2010 Cartmel Show. (Westmorland Gazette)

Opposite, top: The hen-run at Guides Farm. All poultry is now fastened away at night following devastation by a fox. (Paul Nickson)

Opposite, bottom: Cedric admits to being 'mad' about horses, as indicated in these recent scenes at Guides Farm. (Paul Nickson - 2)

Chester was such a character. He could let himself out of the stable and I never knew how, until I hid out of sight one morning and watched. The door was in two halves, with the top half being open the whole of the time. The lower door was bolted, but as I watched he leaned over and fiddled the bar with his mouth. First he had to get the bolt in the right place, or it would not slide along, but he had this worked out to a tee. He then opened his mouth very wide and grabbed the bolt between his teeth to slide it sideways. Then he kicked the door open with his foreleg! He did not like being in the stable because he was such a hardy breed. But if the weather became unbearable, we would stable him for a while so as not to puddle up the land. Yet he would always prefer to be outside – whatever the weather.

You only needed to near his field and shout his name and he would lift his head and come full gallop. One day I noticed that something was wrong when he did not respond to my call and I was really worried. When I got up to him in the field, he looked alright but as I put on the halter and tried to lead him forward he was reluctant to move. After a lot of persuasion, I managed to get him slowly down into the yard and call the veterinary practice. When the vet arrived, he gave him a few tests and thought he had laminitis. I rang my father, who was very knowledgeable with horses. In his younger days, if a fisherman's horse was ill, they used their own methods and medicine and it worked. He didn't agree with the vet and said, "He does not know what he's talking about, mi lad!"

Dad was right. Chester worsened all that day and eventually he could not move a limb and fell down in a heap at the yard gates. I was so upset and rang the vets once again. The second visit was too late. My beautiful Fell pony had picked up a serious infection in the field, a deer tick being found on the sheath of his private parts. Had this been found on the earlier visit from the vets, Chester may well have been saved with antibiotics. He had now got Lymes disease and was suffering. I could not bear to see him like this and asked the vet to put him to sleep. He had lost all colour in his sparkling eyes and the pink flesh in his mouth had gone almost white.

I had to put a large canvas cover over him because he was in the gateway, where anyone who walked past would have seen him lying there and would have found this very upsetting. The following day I got in touch with a friend who owned a JCB digger. He came along and we buried him in the paddock. A couple from Grange, who hardly missed a day coming to see Chester, wrote a lovely tribute. They thought the world of him, as we all did.

A few years later I went along with our daughter Jean and son-in-law Raymond to a horse sale at Clitheroe. When we arrived we went straight to the pens and a black cob caught my eye. Standing about fourteen hands in height, he had an old set of harness on him and he looked very unhappy.

Now and again, someone interested in him would enter his pen and look him over. We noticed a very young lad, who can't have been any older than ten and who lifted up all four feet as we watched. The pony was so quiet that we fell for him right away. We had a long wait as we took our seats at the ringside in the auction mart. Eventually, when the pony was led into the ring, the auctioneer announced him to be sound in every way – ride and drive. The bidding started and we held off at first, then put the last bid in for him. But he was withdrawn because the owner wanted a higher price than what was in the ring.

We were disappointed but after the sale we trudged around the grounds outside the auction mart and came across the owner. Jean was keen for us to buy this horse because he was quiet and just what we wanted. We asked the owner how much he would take for the cob and an agreement was reached.

We called him Charlie. I drive him in harness once a year at our local agricultural show and, although I have never had a first prize with him, I will keep trying. I have recently purchased a very smart Maychester gig and a brand new set of English leather-brass harness. I missed the show in 2012 because of the weather, but hopefully I shall be there with him in future years as he just loves it.

All animals like company and he is not short of it. I also have two pedigree Shetland ponies, one of which is twenty-seven years old and lives with a goat as they do not like to be parted. Another pony was bought by my father and, although Dad was a hundred years old, he always had a soft spot for horses. He managed and lived on his own, and enjoyed sitting in his kitchen to watch this small pony grazing. She is a very quiet and pretty little filly, now four years old, and her breed is an Appaloosa with a pedigree as long as your arm.

Fishing – now as a hobby

I have followed the sands of Morecambe Bay all of my life from leaving school at the age of fourteen and I have fished from a horse and cart for cockles, shrimps, flukes, mussels and whitebait – fishing commercially for a living. These days I do this as a hobby, mainly because there are lots of fish out there to be caught and they are very good for a healthy diet.

All the year round there is one week of high tides and then one of low tides, which are not suitable for fishing, as there are just no fish there to catch. They sense the low tides, which do not reach the upper estuary, and almost all of the fish drop down the Bay into deeper water and lie dormant. When the tide starts to rise they have been without food for several days and they come out onto the sandbanks. Here they feed on small shellfish, either very minute young cockles or the makova, named by the local fishermen and myself as 'hen pennies'.

I just love going out onto these sands and catching our own fish. The nets I set out on the Bay have to be at least three miles or more from the shore. My father taught me a lot about the areas that were best. At one time, setting nets was a very competitive occupation among Flookburgh fishermen and most of them would be at loggerheads with one another. Not today – the Bay is full of fish for the taking, although you still have to take out a licence from the Sea Fisheries and are only allowed to fish in certain areas. Sadly the common fluke – or flounder as they are called – are not so well known away from this area and there is little call for them from the public.

Nowadays there are less than a handful of fishermen and part-timers who set the same type of trap nets as I do. Setting them to stay there against the tides for a number of weeks is quite a task. A large heavy crowbar is put down into the sands to make way for wooden ash stakes. These are about six feet long, straight as a wand and not too thick, and need to go down about three feet.

The stakes are set out in rows about fifteen yards in length parallel to the ridges made by the outgoing tide. They are usually three to four yards apart. The nets can then be run out full length and I start to set by pulling both top and bottom cords over the stakes. The bottom of the net is level with the sand and the top just above knee height. These nets are so fine that they catch both ways with the tide, incoming and outgoing, with the meshes being no less than four-inch so as to

Setting the nets is a painstaking occupation, although the main part of the work starts when the flukes have been caught and then need filleting. (Ian Hughes - 2)

let the immature fish swim on.

Telltale signs of fish coming out onto the sandbanks to feed are called 'shellings' by all the Flookburgh fishermen including myself. Studying an area of sand, you can see the small imprint of a fluke shape. Near to it will be a deposit of fine chewed-up shells, which the fluke have eaten. These are tiny cockles and the small makova, which are pink, white and blue in colour and very delicate. The flukes eat the small fish and spit out the shells. If I find areas with lots of these deposits, I know it's a good place to set my nets.

With inshore fishermen like me, the main part of the work starts once you arrive back home. After unloading the fish from the tractor, I wash the flukes and put them on metal trays to drain and set. I will then usually have a hot drink before I find a comfortable chair at the table in the fish-house and start filleting with a sharp knife on to two or three plastic plates. It can take me up to four hours to fillet one catch, which is then split three ways between John, Mike and myself. Although I do the filleting, my friends help me with both setting the nets and fishing. They are only too pleased when we have a share out and stock up the freezers with the catch, which can last us for quite a while. We just take out a packet when we need one.

The season for fishing for flukes can come to a sudden end if we have severe frost over a period of time. They no longer come up the Bay and hibernate for the winter in deeper and warmer waters. They breed, spawn and then make their way back around March, but at this early time in the year they are as thin as a newspaper. They are best left alone until midsummer, when they will have fattened up on their diet of juicy cockles and the small bivalves. By then they may even find their way into my fishing nets!

Flookburgh fisherfolk at work over a century ago. The figure on the left is using a 'jumbo' to bring the cockles to the surface, while the woman on the right is following with a 'cramb' to spear them and then put them in baskets.

Over: A camera with a 'fish-eye' lens gives a fresh perspective on fishing – and other activities – in the Bay. These views show youngsters examining fluke, the 'brobs' used as markers, a large walk spread out across the sands, and Sandpiper under a wonderful sky. (Ian Hughes - 4)

7. By Special Invitation

Away from Guides Farm and the sands, there have been many wonderful occasions. A very special year was 1999, when in June I was awarded the MBE in the Queen's Birthday Honours. A month later I was invited to attend celebrations marking the 600th anniversary of the link between the Crown and Duchy of Lancaster. In the presence of the Queen and the Duke of Edinburgh, a service at the Priory Church in Lancaster was followed by a luncheon at Ashton Hall. I was sorry that only one ticket was given to each invitee, as I would have loved Olive to have been at my side.

We were both excited when I was notified that the investiture of the MBE would take place at Buckingham Palace on December 2nd. We didn't know how we were going to travel to London, but we were lucky to have some really good friends – Jackie and Geoff Gardner from Worcester. They very kindly offered to drive up to Grange over Sands and take the two of us down to their home to spend the night. We set off very early the next morning to Buckingham Palace with Jackie driving. She was familiar with the journey through London as she had driven this route so often for their family business.

Olive and I could not believe how busy were the roads, with motorcyclists weaving in and out between the fast moving traffic, but Jackie said that this was what they do in London – everything goes at such a pace. "We are not in Grange over Sands now, Ced," she commented. We left our friends' home in Worcester about 6am and arrived at the Palace gates at about 10.15am. Here we joined a queue of vehicles, as each one had to be checked before driving in through the main archway.

As the four of us approached the main entrance to the Palace, we walked slowly up the thickly carpeted steps. Military personnel were placed at intervals to show the way and there were also signs that were plain to see. At the top of the stairway an arrow sign read 'Recipients this way' and guests the other. It was here that we parted company and I was beginning to feel nervous. I followed the other recipients into the waiting area, where we were all briefed on the procedure for the day. I suppose that every one dreams that one day in their lives they will meet the Queen. Well, I must admit that I was one of those people who thought it would never happen to me.

The investiture was held in the Palace Ballroom and started promptly at 11am. I was more nervous now than ever before. As your name was called out, you fell in line with about twenty other recipients. When I was about to go before the Queen, I was hoping that I would remember what to do after following the person in front of me. I was a bag of nerves, but as soon as the Queen spoke to me she put me at my ease. She is just wonderful and I felt humbly proud to be one of her subjects.

Ceremonies of many kinds

In 2001 we had another very nice surprise with a visit from the Mayoress of Grange over Sands. I was given a Civic Award 'in recognition and sincere appreciation for services rendered to the community, life and well-being of the citizens of Grange'. The following year I was given an Honorary Life Membership of the Morecambe Bay Partnership and in 2003 the Outdoor Writers' Guild presented me with the Golden Eagle Award for services to the community. The years 2008 and 2009 saw me honoured as a Tourism Ambassador by the Lancashire and Blackpool Tourism Board with a wonderful ceremony held at Ewood Park Football Stadium in Blackburn.

It's not every day someone names a beer after you, but Moorhouses bestowed that rare honour on me. They stated that the new 4.2 per cent brew was to honour someone 'whose knowledge and devotion to Morecambe Bay had spanned over 44 years'. A second brewery at Morecambe decided that they would like to do the same. Olive and I were invited as special guests at a public house at Lancaster on the banks of the canal. The beer was called 'Sandwalker'.

Every year Olive and I are invited to the University of Central Lancashire at Preston for the award ceremonies for the students, which usually take place in July and again in December. I was given my cap and gown in 1989 and have only missed attending twice in those years. I feel proud to partake in the procession and ceremony, which is held in the Guild Hall at Preston. Olive is a VIP for the day and we are looked after really well.

After the ceremony, Olive joins other guests who are taken back to the university by coach. I stay with the platform party and walk back through the town. We meet and mingle with other Fellows, making new friends, before listening to the Chancellor. This is always followed by an excellent meal and we have now attended this occasion so often that we know most of the staff. These trips are enjoyed so much by us both, as Olive rarely gets much time during the summer to relax, so it is nice for us to take this very little time away for the day – just for a change.

Sandcastles at Morecambe

I have always enjoyed visiting Morecambe from being a teenager and, although changes happen with the times, Olive and I have an exciting feeling about the place. In June 2012 we were both invited by Lancaster and Morecambe City Council to attend the Sandcastle Festival. It was a very chilly day but they made us so welcome and warmed us both up with some hot drinks.

My role on the first day was to meet and greet people and talk about the Bay and the fishing industry. The walk across the Bay is now so widely known that we were not short of people who recognised me and came over to chat. Some of them had been on my previous walks and it was interesting to hear their stories. Unbelievably, one person recognised my thumb stick and came over to the tent. Although there were only small groups of people, they were interested in what I had to tell them of my lifetime on Morecambe Bay.

The day went really well. There were lots of marquees erected, some with entertainment for children such as merry-go-rounds. There was also a festival of music with bands playing from a

The pleasure of a day out to help in judging the outstanding entries at Morecambe Sandcastle Festival. (Morecambe Tourism – 2)

large platform. Crowds of people squatted on the grass enjoying the day and those fabulous views across the Bay. At lunchtime Olive and I were taken across the road to the Winter Gardens for our lunch. This wonderful old building now only serves on certain days as a café and houses bric-a-brac stalls, but the food and the hospitality of the staff was second to none and we were treated like royalty.

The following day the weather was just perfect and brought out the crowds. As we drove into Morecambe, the promenade was bustling with people and we were once again greeted warmly. This was going to be special, as Olive and I had been told that we were to take part in judging the sandcastles and other features and sculptures. Other judges were more familiar with the event as they had done it before, and one or two were specialists on sand art. The exhibits were really outstanding and must have taken hours to prepare. There were large and extra large sandcastles and scary fishes of the Bay including an alligator.

A time was given for the judges to meet up. We were able to walk along the beach and take good notice of all the exhibits before being handed pen and paper to record marks. We had a good look at these fascinating subjects and then put them down in order. The worthy winners were a local couple with two young children who made an enormous sandcastle with a moat filled with water. I was told that they had been the runners-up at this festival in 2011. They were presented with a silver cup and a sum of money, which we all thought was well deserved. This was a day for all to remember as the sun shone down on everyone in Morecambe.

This visit must have been a success because almost two months later came a second invitation for the two of us to attend the Morecambe Seaside Festival at the beginning of September. However, on 11th August

we received a letter from Simon Berry, chairman and managing director of English Lakes, Hotels, Resorts and Venues. It began: "You may recently have read or heard in the press that we have been looking for Cumbrian and North Lancashire residents who regularly go 'above and sometimes beyond' in order to volunteer, aid, assist and help others in and around their own local communities. I am delighted to inform you that you have been nominated personally by people who feel that you deserve recognition for all that you do for them, their families or indeed, for your local community." The letter went on to invite us to a 'Celebration with Community Heroes' in the form of a champagne afternoon tea, which was to be held on the lawns of Low Wood Bay Hotel on the shores of Windermere. This invitation was a lovely surprise, but the date was the same weekend as our earlier invitation to Morecambe Seaside Festival. I therefore decided to ring the Tourism Office and explain the situation. Amazingly, as I was looking in the telephone directory for their number, they rang me. Before I had time to explain about our invitation in the Lakes, they said they were ringing to let us know that they had nominated us and we were not to worry about going to Morecambe. They added, "You both go to this special occasion and enjoy your day."

We did just that – and the day was fabulous. A lot of work must have gone into it to ensure everything ran absolutely smoothly. The food was first class, with lots of champagne to cool everyone down. The sun shone and the setting on the lawns could not have been better – a one off!

8. Queen's Guide no more?

Despite all our recent special occasions, I can't help thinking back to the time over forty years ago when I was involved in a huge project in Morecambe Bay. It was exciting work but it also raised the fear that it might end my role as Queen's Guide.

In 1967 I received an enquiry over the phone from London, asking if it was possible for someone to call on me with a colleague in the next few days to seek my advice. I agreed and two days later a Land Rover drew up at Guides Farm. Two men stepped out and came up the pathway to our front door. They introduced themselves as Bill and Tony from the Water Resources Board in Reading. They were preparing a feasibility study for a possible barrage across the Bay.

Soon after their visit I had more people wanting information about the Bay. Some were putting in tenders for the foundation drilling and wanted to know all about the sands. I gave as much information as I could in such a short time, but it was almost impossible to tell them all about the Bay and its moods. Eventually it was a London firm – a subsidiary of a large construction company – that was chosen to do the drillings.

I had by this time arranged to take two of the bosses out onto the sands by tractor. They arrived by car and were prepared for the weather, equipped with knee boots, leggings, oilskins and helmets. They carried maps and continually looked at them as we made our way out across the vast expanse of the Bay. My tractor was anything but comfortable for my two passengers, with only a wooden platform that was built out on the back. This was to carry my fishing gear but was not really suitable for passengers. I was pointing out different areas and types of sand as I drove along. Occasionally they would ask me to stop and they would then jump from the back of the tractor. They asked me lots of questions. "Are there many areas which change frequently?" they enquired as they paddled up and down on the sands just like children would have done.

After a time they seemed satisfied, although in my mind they had seen very little of this huge area of sands and water – not having gone right out into the Bay. They decided that we should make back to Guides Farm and at this stage I had no idea of what they were planning or what part I was to play in it. Back by the warm fire in the living room, we sat over a cup of tea and chatted about the next move. I assisted them in finding a base from which to work – a small plot of land ideal for their job and belonging to Edward and Maureen Burrow at West Plain Farm in Flookburgh. We needed to discuss the preparations required before any work could start and a hut for stores and equipment would have to be erected.

Electricity had to be laid on and the telephone brought in. Luckily there was already a tap with fresh water on hand. I was thanked for all I had done for them and they asked me if I would help them out from time to time. I was busy with my fishing and my guided walks through the summer months, but I did not mind taking them out onto the sands if they gave me prior notice.

Whatever took place on the sands always interested me. As I went about my fishing, I would take the longer route through Allithwaite and down onto the main road to Flookburgh, just to pass the new site and see what progress was being made. Permanent staff had been appointed and were waiting for the drilling equipment to be brought up from London.

At last I received a telephone call from Northolt in Middlesex from the drilling manager asking me if I would be willing to help him. He said that he hoped to start work in the Bay in early August and that a site agent would be coming up in the next few days. He added that he and his wife would need accommodation and asked if Olive and I could find them somewhere to stay in Grange over Sands. As work progressed, I would be needed more often, sometimes to take a couple of technicians out to the line of the proposed barrage.

If we went out on the low tides and the weather was fine, my tractor wheel marks would still show quite clearly the following day. This gave them confidence – too much in fact. One day I arrived to find that the site agent, along with some of his technicians, had ventured out onto the sands in one of their own ex-army wagons and had followed the tracks made by my tractor the previous day. What they did not realise was that the tides were on the rise. In thinking of going out into the Bay on their own, assuming that everything was simple and straightforward, they would very soon learn a tough lesson.

The next time I was asked to go down onto the site, I noticed a huge circular concrete platform was finished and wagons carrying steel girders of various lengths and sizes were being unloaded there. Soon, the first drilling tower was being assembled and now I knew the purpose of the concrete platform.

I was asked to go down to the site one morning. As I walked across to the site office the agent said, "Good morning, Mr. Robinson. What's the earliest time you can get us out onto the sands?" This depended on whereabouts in the Bay they wanted to be. As I leaned over the table, I glanced at a map with marks and numbers, A6, A7 and so on, which represented bore holes. Surveyors had earlier marked out these points with wooden posts.

I knew all the area really well because I had been over it so many times. For me to describe the Bay on the line of the proposed barrage was in fishermen's terms like a duck's back – simple but straightforward thinking. The longer stretch across the centre of the Bay was the highest and driest on low tides, with the east and west sides being very much lower with frequent changes and faster tidal currents.

They told me that they wanted to go to the area marked A1. In this area the force of the tide, both outgoing and incoming, was at its worst and most dangerous. We could go to the other marker points much more easily than this one, which was in the lowest part of the Bay on the west side near to the River Leven – the main channel. Here the tide ebbs late and comes back sooner, leaving only about four hours of working time.

I had now seen the new drilling tower getting near completion and it was my own belief that it would never stay upright out there. But I felt they ought to know what they were doing and whether it would work. By this time, I had been asked if I could find some local lads to work on the rigs and so half a dozen from Flookburgh started on the site. My first job was to take one of these lads to help me mark out the route on the sands, putting in wooden stakes about one hundred yards apart.

Following wheel marks on the sands can be a great help in finding one's way. It can also be very dangerous, especially if it is not realised that the tide is on the rise. (Ian Hughes)

We wrapped each one of them with DayGlo, a brilliant orange-coloured material that could be seen in the dark when the lights from the tractor eventually caught them. They were even visible in fog. After a while, routes were marked out from the site and to all the drilling rigs.

The big move

Two bulldozers with caterpillar tracks - massive machines – had been brought in from a local plant hire firm to tow the drilling tower over the sands. Long wire ropes were shackled from each bulldozer to the front corners of the huge tower. It was 80ft high and was constructed of iron girders with four large hollow wheels in metal, similar to those seen on the front wheel of the old-fashioned steamrollers. Although it could be towed quite easily across level sands, changes of direction were a bit of a problem.

One bulldozer had to take the strain whilst the other one slackened off. Stops were frequent on the rough knobbly sand and with the constant changes of direction we found that nearly all the nuts and bolts had worked loose. It took a long time for them to be tightened up. By now we were feeling anxious, because we knew that even if things went without any snags it would take us most of the time between the tides to get the tower to its site – a distance of four miles. We just managed it, and in spite of everything the tower stood safely, ready to be put into its final position. All this time I had been leading the way with my old tractor. Following at the rear was a four-wheel drive, ex-army vehicle carrying the bosses and the drillers and labourers. They had brought with them perforated sheets of metal, approximately 10ft long by 8ft wide – the type used by the military in the last war to enable transport to drive over boggy areas without getting stuck. These were laid on the sand to carry the wheeled vehicles over the worst places and could then be picked up and moved forward. They were eventually put under the tower.

Orders were given as we drove the last few yards. The army truck went ahead and then halted – and now the men were flitting around like flies. I had my eye on my watch and kept my tractor clear. I then walked over to the spot where the caterpillar tractors were to pull the drilling tower on to the metal mats. These mats were moved about until they were in the correct position and then instructions were given to the caterpillar drivers to take the strain, slowly ease forward and put the tower into place. "Easy does it," cried the gaffer, and then "Stop!" He was all smiles, probably thinking that the worst part was over.

I looked again at my watch and realised that we had got barely enough time to get out of this low area with the caterpillars, as they could not travel as fast as my old tractor and the army wagon. Our outward tracks were still showing clearly and I told the drivers to be making along them. They would soon be on much higher and safer ground where they would be clear of the tide for a long time. After doing a few necessary jobs, we caught up with them.

These caterpillar tractors intrigued me, as they could go just about anywhere. I stayed alongside them because dark was closing in. The army wagon raced over the sands for home and we could see the spray from the wheels until it was away out of sight. By the time we reached base, everyone except the boss had gone home. We parked our vehicles for the night and then I was called over to the office to confirm times for the next day and to discuss what we were to expect.

As the tide comes into the Bay twice in twenty-four hours we would miss the night tide. The next day we could not leave the base until 2.30pm, but then we could get straight out to the rig without any problems. The bosses decided that we should all travel in the army wagon. I was to leave my tractor on the site. By now everyone was anxious to see how the rig had stood up to the force of the tides. This seemed to be the sole topic of conversation. I had my own opinion based on past experiences, but I was there simply with a job to do – a responsible one too as turned out to be the case.

The time came for us to set off out to the drilling tower rig and everyone climbed aboard the army wagon – the drilling manager, the site agent, the drillers and what were called their second men. We held tight as we heard the engine start up knowing that we were in for a bumpy ride. We went down the track, but once on the sands the going was much more comfortable than riding on my old tractor. I was thinking it might not perhaps be as reliable, as we were indeed later to discover.

First one and then another looked out from under the canvas cover of the wagon to see if they could catch a glimpse of the rig. I had the feeling that something was wrong as it came into sight. It looked to me as if it was leaning over at quite an angle and I pointed this out to the site manager who was alongside me. "No, Cedric, it's an optical illusion," he said. I did not think so. I was so used to looking long distances over the sands and I was sure the tower was no longer upright. No one could convince me otherwise. The route was well marked all the way, so the driver had no worries on that score and we were soon nearing the rig. I had in my mind's eye what we would see when we got there and asked the driver not to go too near. The tide would have scoured round the rig, as it does with anything left on the sands. Even with something as small as a bucket, it has the same effect.

After finding that the rig was indeed at an angle, we were unable to get onto it. The tide had scoured round it to such an extent that it was now sitting in a huge waterlogged hole. Not only had the sand beneath been washed away – the whole structure had dropped down below the wheels. The bosses made a quick survey and decided that if it was possible to straighten up the rig, they might still be able to drill from it. I did not think so, but now for action. Decisions had to made quickly as we had only four hours between the tides. Most of us would now have to return to base, leaving just two men out there. They could do nothing at this stage. Everyone at base was waiting to hear our news, but it was not for us to publicise or criticise so we gave them the bare facts and waited for our instructions.

I was to take the two drivers with their caterpillars out to the rig as quickly as possible. This was going to be a race against time. I checked my tractor for fuel and oil and then we drove out of the site and over the marsh, followed by the two caterpillars. In the meantime, several lorry loads of stone had been ordered from a local quarry. As soon as the caterpillars were safely at the rig, I returned to base to meet the lorry drivers. They had previously been out on the marsh, but this time they had actually to drive out on the sands – which was a new experience for them. I knew I could get them out there safely, but the salt water in the shallow dykes would throw up a spray. This would play havoc with their braking systems once they were back on the road, so they would have to be extra careful.

The route was easy to follow because our wheel marks were still showing from our earlier trips. I drove backwards and forwards to make sure the convoy of wagons were alright and told the drivers that in no way would they sink. We had two caterpillars on hand – but they had another job to do.

The first lorry driver was asked to go as near as possible to the scoured-out hole around the rig and then tip his load. He had to keep on the move and I watched the sand quiver as the stone disappeared. A caterpillar pushed the stone into the gaping hole but it vanished almost straight away. By now the lorries were going round in a circle, not daring to stop and keeping clear of each other's wheel marks so as not to soften up the sand around the rig. It was an impossible task – a load of stone went nowhere and just disappeared into the gaping holes.

With the amount of stone we had available and with time running out, we decided to work on one side only, instead of trying to fill in all round, so that we could get onto the rig to see what damage had been done. After a quick inspection the boss thought that it would be possible – or at least worth a try – to attach long wire cables from a position high up on the structure of the rig. This was at last done, and every one of us stood well back. Instructions were clearly given for the two caterpillars to take up the slack of the wires. Making sure that they both pulled evenly together, they started to move but the suction in the sand around the base of the rig had too strong a hold and would not release it – even to the power of the two caterpillars.

Disaster!

The result was catastrophic. As the 80ft tower and its equipment broke into pieces and hurtled to the ground, everyone ran for their lives. The noise was terrible, as metal girders and steel sections were breaking up – one part crashing against the other. It was very frightening but luckily no one was hurt. All we could do now was salvage anything we could easily lay our hands on and do so as quickly as possible. Time was short – the caterpillars must be first on their way home, then the lorry drivers, who all of this time had been moving slowly round, not daring to stop. I knew they would be only too glad to go. I jumped on my tractor, ready to lead the convoy to higher ground and safety. It was now almost dark and we had to use our lights to see the tracks and markers.

One elderly wagon driver, who had lived all his life in the area, said to me, "Well, mi lad, I've often wondered what it was like out here, but now I've seen it – once is enough for me!" He meant that he wouldn't come out again at any price.

We all reached base safely. The lorry drivers thanked me for my help and drove off to their homes. We parked the rest of the vehicles for the night and I made my way to the office as usual. I had already worked out the times when we could go out on the sands the following day. However, as there was a lot of valuable equipment where the rig had collapsed, I was asked to go out with a strong lad from the village, following the next tide, to guard against any would-be pirates! This meant going out in the middle of the night. I took my tractor and 'Boxer' John Wright. That was my mate's nickname – he was and still is a right good sort and could handle himself as a boxer. We also needed my tractor because while we were there we were going to salvage whatever we could.

We had not been at the rig long when I could see lights coming towards us out of the night. As they drew nearer we heard the noise of their tractor engine and their voices. The visitors (or pirates) must have been surprised to find someone already there. On seeing 'Boxer' Wright, who was as strong as an ox, they changed their minds, turned their tractor around pretty sharpish and made off into the night. If there had been any trouble, my mate could have easily dealt with them but we weren't looking for a fight and it didn't come to that. We never found out who they were.

We had a flask of coffee and a few sandwiches with us and now we could relax for a short while and have a natter over our drink. Before long, daylight would break and we would be better able to see what we could salvage before the turn of the tide. We got on well with the job and then began to think about making tracks for home. The tide couldn't be far away, so we knew we had better get moving.

Piece after piece had been dragged from the heap of twisted metal and loaded onto the tractor. Smaller pieces and some equipment were packed onto the back and we made our way home. It was still very early. I looked at my watch and it said a quarter to seven.

The sand was very flat for the first mile or so and we made good going. The sooner we got back the better, as we would be able to get a few hours sleep before the next tide ebbed. By my

Morecambe Bay can assume an utterly different character at night. This striking photograph captures both the starry sky and pinpoints of light from distant settlements. (Paul Nickson)

reckoning that would be about half past three in the afternoon. All was quiet as we parked the tractor. It was too early for anyone to have started work, so I dropped 'Boxer' off on my way home, arranging to pick him up again at one o'clock after I had had something to eat. Later, of course, everyone wanted to know how we had fared during the night out on the sands. When we told them of our visitors, there was a great deal of speculation as to who the would-be pirates were, but it had been too dark for us to see them – or where they went.

The salvage operation began. This was to be our final visit to the broken rig and the last to that particular area for a long time. I was asked to accompany a bulldozer with wire ropes and two tractors with trailers to load up whatever we could salvage. We hoped to clear the area completely this time. The power of the bulldozer was amazing. The wire ropes were fastened to the girders, which were pulled clear in no time by the huge machine. Eventually everything that could be saved had been recovered, and all that was left was the gaping hole and a small patch of stone.

We coupled up the bulldozer to the long girders and set off on the return journey. I stayed alongside as the driver had to take it very slowly with this load. The girders gouged into the sand making great furrows – slowing our progress still further. Time was slipping by and I waved the tractor drivers to go on ahead. "Follow the tracks," I shouted to them, "Don't try to take any short cuts either. There's plenty under the sand that's tried that!"

After a while I realised that we could not make it with this load. The tide would be coming in before we managed to get out, so I suggested to the driver that we take the girders up onto high ground and leave them to be collected later. After all, they were not much good for anything now other than scrap. The tide would not reach and scour round them on the higher ground, so we unloaded them on a rise and left them there in order for us to make it back safely. The girders could be brought back next day when we would have all the time between the tides to do the job.

I had thought that the whole team would have been disheartened with this disaster, but no – the spirit and determination of those lads was wonderful to see. They were not going to allow even such a major setback to prevent the progress of the survey.

Taming the Bay

A great friend of ours, W E Swale, in his 1969 book *Grange over Sands: The Story of a Gentle Township*, describes the work of the survey and the problems of the task in which I had become so closely involved:

'Towns north of a line from Hest Bank to, say, Ulverston, face the possibilities of the construction of a barrage which would drastically alter their physical surroundings. The object of the original scheme was merely to carry a railway line along the top of the dam, a source of cooling water for electricity power stations, land reclamation and above all – water storage. If it does nothing else, the present feasibility study has aroused great interest and been a minor source of local employment. The study, estimated to cost around £500.000, to be finished in 1971 is proceeding under the overall direction of the Water Resources Board in Reading. The combined skill of a number of specialist firms is being called upon so that every conceivable aspect of a complex problem may be exhaustively examined.

'Consulting engineers are dealing with constructional work, surveyors have made aerial and hydrographical observations. Experts in soil mechanics had sunk 35 boreholes, reaching depths of 300ft. A scale model of the waters and shores of Morecambe Bay had been made in which simulated tides will, it is hoped, predict the long term effects of the barrage, as far down as Barrow Harbour. It is certain that all these Bay explorers will have read accounts of the extraordinary high tide of 27th December 1857, which exceeded by twelve feet anything ever recorded before or since, or the great gale of 27th February 1903, when, in the early morning hours, the down train was blown over as it crossed the Leven Sands viaduct, fortunately without loss of life. These accidents prove that Morecambe Bay will not be easily tamed.'

He was right about the difficulties, as our first disastrous attempt had already proved, but the work went on. New plans had to be thought out and many journeys were made out onto the sands, trying out different ideas and techniques. In some areas it was decided to use stone as the foundation on which to build the steel scaffolding. In other places where the tidal flow was stronger, it was found that mattresses of perforated sheet steel laid over sheets of hessian were the most effective.

My chief job was choosing the routes out to the new areas, marking them and visiting the drilling rigs with the bosses. Mostly, I acted as their guide and I had nothing to do with the actual drilling. When a new base for a rig was being laid, it was most important that everything possible should be known about the sands and tides in that area. This was where my experience of the Bay was most useful to them.

I felt I had a great responsibility for the safety of both personnel and plant, but what a good firm and a grand lot of lads these were to work with. At first we were nearly all strangers to one another, but as time progressed we got on well together. Scaffolding firms were soon erecting drilling towers up and down the Bay.

They had to have information about the flow of the tides in each area where it was proposed to put up a tower. The job was formidable, as all the equipment had to be taken out on four-wheel drive trailers, hired from a local firm in Kendal. I marked out all routes where I knew the sands would be safe for some time. When I was sure there would be no great change along these routes, I would give the drivers the times of the tides and tell them when they could go out and return safely. If the weather was changeable, or if there was any chance of fog, I would then take them out and guide them from my tractor. In this way serious trouble was avoided.

However, there was one close shave. We had a solid week of fog. I had given one of the lads directions for getting back to base with his tractor, telling him to follow my tracks as the wheel marks still showing on the sands. Unfortunately another set of tracks confused him and he followed the wrong ones, which were making back down the Bay towards the incoming tide. 'Boxer' and I were on our way home when we spotted him, so we put on full speed and soon had him back on the right tracks. "Well," said 'Boxer', "He'd have been a goner had we not just seen him at that time." He was lucky and lived to tell the tale.

There is just nothing as bad, or as frightening, as being out on Morecambe Bay in the fog, even if like me you have been on the sands all your life. But as long as you take notice of the nature of the Bay and respect it, you should not come to any harm.

Tempting providence

A large number of men were needed to work on the drilling towers and plans had to be worked out for getting them out to these rigs and back again to the shore. One of the firm's vans was used to bring the men into base from their homes or digs. I then had to take them out to the drilling platforms on my tractor between the tides and bring them back to base after their stint was over – in all kinds of weather. It was a most uncomfortable ride for the men, especially when they were tired from their hard work on the rigs.

The firm decided to buy a DUKW – the manufacturers' code for an amphibious landing craft used in the last war. Although it may have been old, it was a comfortable ride with six-wheel drive

and could get out to any area of the Bay at speed. It did quite well as a personnel carrier, but Morecambe Bay is different to other sites where a DUKW would be operating in deep water right off the shore. Out in the Bay you could be in the river where the water was fast flowing, and then suddenly find yourself in shallow water. As the front of the vehicle was lighter than the rear end, it would spin round and at first we could not solve this problem. Eventually we found that we had to go out when the tide was at its full, or wait until it had ebbed so that the vehicle could ride on its wheels.

As the DUKW was so big, the men started using it to move all sorts of equipment out to the rigs. I grew more and more worried as I saw bigger and bigger loads being taken out. I felt they were tempting providence.

Early one morning I was out on the sands, taking men out to two drilling towers over on the west side of the Bay, just out from Aldingham village. The DUKW was transporting men and equipment to and from the rigs on the Flookburgh side of the fast flowing River Leven. On my way back to the shore, I could see the vehicle quite clearly speeding towards us and making for the rigs. I had just left the sands and knew that the tide was due. I wondered what were they doing out there this late on the tide.

It was the highest of tides and it was very fast running. The vehicle was loaded with heavy metal scaffolding and there were half a dozen men on board. They must have mistaken the time of the tide. When the DUKW drove into the river, the tidal bore hit it with such a force, turning it round with water passing in the rear end and the front coming up fast. The men were all huddled together at the fore end completely at the mercy of the tide.

At last they had the sense to throw the scaffolding into the river to relieve the weight. The vehicle righted itself, but only after these lads had been more scared than at any time in their lives. They had plenty of power in the engine to make their way back to Chapel Island, which was much higher up the Bay, but were now on the wrong side of the River Leven channel. When they tried to cross the river, the force of the tide turned them round again. They did eventually get away from it, helped by the speed of the vehicle, and were able to make back to base at Flookburgh.

Later they told us about their alarming experience, saying that one of the drillers, a coloured lad, went white with fright when he saw the danger they were in. He got his own back on the other lads and said that they went green! At home that night I could not sleep for thinking of this very near tragedy. I was afraid they would not be so lucky another time, so I wrote out a list of jobs for which I thought it was safe to use the DUKW. Everyone agreed, so a list of do's and don'ts was put up on posters, one copy in the front of the vehicle and the other in the main office. After that the DUKW was used sensibly without any more trouble.

The 80ft high rigs used in the late 1960s for surveying the proposed Morecambe Bay barrage were awesome structures. Cedric greatly enjoyed working on this project. (Barrow News & Mail)

Rough conditions

Drilling was now going well from the rigs based at Flookburgh, but more were needed at the other side of the Bay. The foreshore at Bolton-le-Sands was chosen for the base from which to start the work of building new rigs. As soon as they were built, the men were brought in from Flookburgh on the DUKW to work on them. This meant crossing the River Kent. The biggest problem was getting the men to the rigs when the tide was at its full in early mornings. To save time, it was decided to take them round by road to Morecambe, where a fisherman I knew very well would meet them at the jetty and take them to the rigs in his boat. I was able to go along with the men and help with the unloading, which we found difficult when the sea was choppy.

Rough conditions also made it tricky for the men to climb from the boat to the rig. A row of old motor tyres hung at the right height solved the problem to some extent. Each rig had an inflatable life raft, fitted with an outboard engine in case of an emergency, so the safety of the men was well to the fore. There was also a walkie-talkie radio system that saved a lot of time and could save lives too.

The only occasion when one of the inflatables had to be used was when the men on a drilling rig near Morecambe thought they felt it move as they were pulling up the casing. Word was passed to base by radio and very soon I was on my way round to the jetty at Morecambe, where I found my good friend Ernie Nicholson in his boat waiting for me.

As we neared the rig I could see the three men sitting in the rubber dinghy, anchored to the ramp that led up to the rig. They were so glad to see us; it couldn't have been so pleasant sitting in an open boat, maybe thinking about the rig that had collapsed earlier. We took them back to base and when the tide ebbed I took the boss out on my tractor to survey the damage.

Looking at the structure of the rig, it seemed that very little had happened. When the men had felt it move slightly, the tide would have been scouring round the base and the rig would have been straining. This drew the metal casing up out of the sand, causing slight movement of the rig. There was plenty of time to do what was needed to stabilise the structure. Stone was on hand, stockpiled on the shore for such an emergency. As soon as the tide had left the area, work started on filling in the base. It was soon finished and the lads were able to work on the rig again the following day.

Now that all the rigs were in working order and drilling was going ahead, I could bring my tractor back across the sands to Flookburgh. The rivers Kent and Keer had to be forded, and at that time I knew a good shallow crossing of the Kent well up in the Bay where I could get through quite easily. I should have been able to make the first of the journeys in daylight if I got moving.

After fording the river up near Grange, I was glad to be closer to home, as I could see fog closing in fast. It was rolling up the Bay and blotting out all sight of any landmarks. I had now to use my knowledge of the area, as I had no tracks to follow. Although I hadn't far to go, a short distance on the sands in fog seems never ending – it is a nightmare. I switched on my tractor lights, but they just made the fog and darkness look like a black wall. I was better without them.

I was glad to get up on to higher ground, when finally I came across some tracks on the sand. I got down from my tractor and had a closer look at them. Yes, they were my very own tracks. I found a marker that I had put in a few days earlier and knew that I was on the way to the marsh at Flookburgh. Was I glad to get home that Friday night!

Missing lads

No one went out to the rigs on Saturdays or Sundays. Little did we know that five lads – part time fishermen – had sailed down the River Lune from Lancaster one Friday evening. They had packed up their sandwiches and a couple of flasks of tea and then went to do a night of fishing. They had two boats in which they sailed out into the Morecambe Bay. It came in foggy and they lost their way.

They carried no compass and had no idea of where they were at all. They were too cold to sleep and they were scared. By the next day all their food had gone. They had a can of water but they had to go careful with it, not knowing how long they would be out there for before someone came to their rescue.

Saturday and Sunday came and went, and the situation grew more frightening by the minute. It was given out on the radio that five fishermen were missing in Morecambe Bay, but in such fog it was of no use any other boats going out to look for them. Since the fishermen had no radio with them they didn't even know whether or not they had been missed.

On the Monday morning I had to go out across the Bay on my tractor to take some drillers out to one of the rigs, about a mile or so from Morecambe and as far as I could go before coming across rather deep water. I left at six o'clock from Flookburgh and it took me much longer than usual, as the fog was still fairly thick. I landed the men without any trouble and then turned my tractor in a wide circle to start my journey back over the Bay. I thought I could just make out something in the fog and it looked like a boat. I managed to get closer with my tractor, and then I could see that there were in fact two boats with the missing lads standing round the masts. The water was about three feet deep and I was able to drive in and pull alongside.

I had heard about the lads on the radio when I was crossing the sands and thought that they would have been much lower down the Bay. When I got close to them I noticed that they were as black as the fire back. This was now Monday morning and they had been out since Friday night.

These fisher lads recognised me at once, because only a couple of months earlier my son Robert and his pal Larry had purchased an old lifeboat from them and I had had to take them round to Lancaster in my car. "Bloody hell, Ced," they cried as I approached, "Aren't we glad to see you! Where the hell are we?" Now, when it's foggy and hazy you can sometimes still see the sun coming up above the haze. I knew exactly where they were and suggested they should sail down with the ebb tide for about ten minutes and then make into the sun. With a bit of luck, I knew that they should make it somewhere near to Morecambe jetty.

It was in all the newspapers the next day. Wasn't it lucky for them that they came across me that Monday morning, as the fog stayed with us in the Bay for over a week?

The Morecambe Bay barrage may have been shelved, but there have been other noticeable changes. An offshore windfarm near Walney Island now adds a new look to the horizon. (Paul Nickson)

Opposite: A barrage would unquestionably have changed plant life over a vast area. The magic of the shoreline, seen here on a distinctly chilly morning, would have been lost. (Paul Nickson)

Sink or swim!

Equipment was needed at short notice on one of the rigs close to Morecambe. Ernie was out in the Bay fishing for shrimps, but my friend Larry, who is a most obliging chap, had offered to give me a hand if ever I needed help. So I got in touch with him and we soon had the goods aboard his boat at Cart Lane. The rig was about half a mile from Morecambe and we got there without any trouble, but Larry was a bit late on the tide. We unloaded all the equipment and then turned the boat round for home. There was now a breeze coming up and quite a lot of surf, and when we got nearer to where the river was ebbing there was even more surf. Every time I looked round, great rollers were coming over the boat. We were both soaked to the skin and feeling cold. We were just too late on the tide and we were at full throttle with the front of the boat right up out of the water.

I thought – well, it's sink or swim! I'm no boatman, admittedly, but I'd never sailed like this in my life. The front went up and the rear went down. I was now on my hands and knees – no, not praying – but I couldn't stand up so I got the only lifejacket from up front and left Larry to the sailing of the boat.

I do not know the first thing about boats, but I've travelled almost every inch of the Bay when the tide has been out and know every dyke and hollow in it. Larry yelled at me that he would make for Humphrey Head to keep in deeper water. As the boat careered towards the headland, I thought that we would certainly run aground. I was more than glad when we did, as the bottom of the boat ran out of water. I now knew exactly where we were. We anchored the boat and had to walk the five miles home – but to me that was much better and safer than riding the waves in Larry's boat.

The story isn't over yet though. The very next day Larry asked if I would take him and our son Robert out to his boat on my tractor. I knew exactly where it had run aground, but Larry was a bit late in turning up. Eventually we were on our way going across the sands from Flookburgh. When we arrived at the water's edge the tidal bore had just gone past the boat, but I was able to drive into the tide with my tractor. I quickly drew alongside to enable Larry and Robert to jump into the boat.

By now the water was just covering the front wheels of my tractor, almost three feet deep but flowing very fast. I drove back out away from the tide and stopped on higher ground to watch them. They started the engine right away – too early in fact. They should have lain at anchor for a while to let the sandbanks cover. Instead they moved off and ran into a sandbank, which threw them aground yet again and this time they were broadside on to the tide.

It looked to me as if the tide was likely to tip them over. As for what Larry did next, he deserved a medal. He had a plank of wood on board and there was a wide lip across this old metal lifeboat. So he put the plank under this lip with the other end of it several feet out from the boat and over the fast-flowing tidal water. He then crawled along this plank to try and bring the boat level with his weight and movement. He succeeded and the boat was freed, so he scrambled back along the plank and they sailed off for Grange over Sands. Was I glad, as I was able to watch this from a safe distance and could see the danger they were in. It took my breath away.

A project in the past?

By the time of this adventure some of the rigs out from Flookburgh had almost finished their drillings and before long the job of dismantling would have to begin. I had enjoyed the whole period of my part-time employment with the firm and made many new friends. None of us was looking forward to the day when the work would come to an end. I can honestly say that, although my job held a lot of responsibility, I did find that this was really appreciated by everyone who worked on the survey.

In 1972, after five years of study, the Water Resources Board concluded that Morecambe Bay could be used for freshwater storage. Several different schemes were outlined. A full barrage twelve miles long, reaching from Hest Bank to Baycliffe, near Aldingham, and carrying a dual carriageway road, would cost an estimated £69 – 73 million. A major disadvantage of this plan would have been the probable extent of silting on the seaward side, putting at risk major parts such as Heysham Harbour, Fleetwood and Barrow.

The Board did not, in fact, recommend at that stage whether or not the Bay should be developed. Since then the project appears to have been shelved for lack of funds, so all that is now in the past but is not forgotten. Since all the forms of water storage examined by the Board are feasible in engineering terms, sometime in the future the barrage could become a reality.

W E Swale summed up the position in his book: 'If the barrage is ever built, the livelihood of a hardy, modest and extremely knowledgeable race of men will largely disappear. The emergence of a 40 square mile inland lake has exhilarating possibilities, not only for water sport, but also for other types of fishing. The broad waters that have for centuries been known in local records have their hazards. Changes in plant and animal life, notably in the possible growth of sedges and rushes around the shores of the lake, may pose yet unforeseen problems. It is more than likely that the present generation of fishermen may still be able to use their particular skills in the service of subsequent users of (or sufferers from) the Great Morecambe Lake.'

9. Doing what we have always done

If the Morecambe Bay barrage had come to pass, my job as Queen's Guide would obviously have become obsolete. I would have had to learn one end of a boat from the other, buying a small fleet of them and hiring them out on the new lake. What a thought! This would seem the only way of earning a living that would have remained open to me, but it could never have compensated for my memories of the past. I would have lost something that had been part of me all of my life. My livelihood, my constant challenge, the thousands of people I have met over the years, my second home – the sands.

Happily there have in fact been few changes down the years, although there was one surprise in 2010. Each year a Trustees' meeting is held at the private office of Lord Hugh Cavendish's estate at Holker Hall. He is chairman of the Guide over Sands Trust and it is here that I take my annual report of numbers and names of all the people I have taken across the Bay in the season. At the meeting in 2010, Lord Cavendish surprised me when he announced that he wanted Olive and I to hand over the dates and times of the Bay walks to Grange over Sands Town Council. They would take over their running and make a charge of £1 per person. I could hardly believe this was happening, as Olive and I had been choosing the dates and arranging these walks for almost fifty years for free. Organisers would have to pay £1 per head up front and if the weather meant that I had to cancel a walk the money would not be refunded. Some organisations reluctantly paid up, others withheld and many smaller charitable organisations could not afford to participate and cancelled altogether.

Golden wedding celebrations in 2011, with the cake appropriately featuring icing in the shape of a book. (Paul Nickson - 2)

Running the Tourist Information Office in Grange over Sands was becoming doubtful – it was said that the Council could not afford to keep it open. Fortunately means were found and it is now being run by a very obliging voluntary staff with one local person, Lynn, whom I know well and who was born in Grange over Sands. Olive and I are much happier now. We are doing what we have always done, answering the phone and giving out the dates and times of the Morecambe Bay walks as well as lots of information that is always appreciated.

Our happiness was increased when in November 2011 we celebrated our golden wedding anniversary at the Ravenstown Club in Flookburgh. I invited the Houghton Weavers, who have become a landmark on the music scene in the North West and beyond. Their unique blend of music and humour captures the imagination of young and old alike. I first met up with them on one of my cross-Bay walks and have since followed their concerts locally at the Victoria Hall in Grange over Sands and the Coronation Hall in Ulverston. They are a very popular group with many followers and their concerts are usually a sell out.

Our son Robert, who was at that time the landlord of the Crown Inn at Flookburgh, kindly offered to cater for all 150 of our guests, friends, relatives and neighbours with a buffet fit for a queen. Our eldest son Bill, his wife Jackie and our daughter Diane brought along a most beautifully decorated cake and placed on top in the shape of a book was a picture of us both in icing. We all had a most wonderful and memorable evening.

Olive and I still enjoy giving lectures and showing slides of life and times on Morecambe Bay. We are a jolly good team and it has been said that our shows are very enjoyable. We are like two comedians. I know for sure, Olive must surely not be the youngest projectionist in Cumbria at 87 years young – but she loves it!

We would like to cut down on the travelling now, especially in the winter months. At the end of a lecture and slide show, the audience show such an interest and many of them come over to us to talk and ask questions. However, we are often miles from home and I have all the equipment to carry out and pack into my car. This makes it late for us driving home, but we have made lots of new friends through these meetings.

We are proper home birds. We absolutely love living in Grange over Sands and looking out and studying the sands of Morecambe Bay. We have never had a holiday away and have not really found the time or a need for one. We are both content and happy at what we are doing – and have done for the past fifty years.

Part 2

Golden Anniversary Tributes

Terry Marsh has many times crossed the Bay with Cedric but it has always seemed a new experience. He took this photograph on one such occasion, when the weather was at its finest.

10. Memories of many kinds

Someone everyone would want as a friend

Terry Marsh

I first crossed Morecambe Bay in the 1990s, the day after Cedric had his heart bypass operation. When Gren Harrison, the Senior Fisheries Officer, turned up in place of Cedric, who was, understandably, somewhat indisposed, I quipped, "What kind of an excuse is that for not being here?" Fifteen years later that particular chicken came home to roost, with a vengeance.

In the meantime, and on many occasions since, I've crossed the Bay with Cedric, and such is his knowledge, understanding and basic human compassion that each crossing was a new experience in spite of the fundamental similarity. Out there, in the middle of that Bay, a place all the more stigmatised by the many deaths that have occurred there, you suddenly come to realise how life-dependent you are on this one man and his knowledge of the sands. It's eerie, overwhelming, threatening, and yet appealing and exciting, all at the same time. From its wooded edge, the Bay beckons like an impatient child, drawing you into its huge embrace.

The magic of those experiences is one of the reasons why, when I was faced with choosing a topic for a Master of Arts degree at Lancaster, I latched on to the history of the Guides to Morecambe Bay Sands. Among this elite band, Cedric ranks as one of the longest serving, having taken up office in October 1963, a time pre-computers, mobile phones, world-wide internet connections and a host of other things that today we take for granted. Mind you, it has been argued that television was better in those days!

Cedric is also the last in a long, and mostly illustrious, line of Guides to the sands; local fishermen, who through the 19th and 20th centuries took up the office and put their lives on the line to secure the safe passage of travellers across the sands.

Quite when the first Guides appeared is now lost from record. For centuries it was the responsibility of the monks at Furness and Cartmel to provide some form of guiding service, and it is reasonably certain that it was they who eventually appointed 'official' Guides. Certainty on this point comes from the fact that as part of the process of the Dissolution of the Monasteries by Henry VIII, he ordered a valuation of the monasteries, which became known as the Valor Ecclesiasticus. In it two Guides appear as such, William Gate and John Harteley; the one for the Kent Estuary, the other for the Leven Sands.

The earliest 'Guide' who can safely be identified is a man named Edmondson, who appears in records of 1501, but before then, although there is evidence that the abbeys did provide a service, the identity of the incumbents was lost when the chartularies were destroyed at the time of the Dissolution. But, by any standards, today's Guide to the Kent Sands – there is another for the Leven Sands even today – comes from a long pedigree of sand pilots.

Cedric, supported by his lovely wife, Olive, is a remarkable man; someone everyone would want as a friend. He is unfailingly amiable and polite, when at times he would be more than justified in being quite the opposite, but, in spite of his advancing years, still rattles across the sands at a pace that many younger folk have difficulty keeping up with. What makes him especially charming, for those few who get to know him, is an innocence of all things and places beyond his domain. For someone who has been honoured by, and met, the Queen, this is quite remarkable. Even going to Keswick is like going to a foreign country for Cedric and Olive; they have been, of course, and do actually travel widely, but they are very home-centric.

A few years ago, Cedric was given an award by the Outdoor Writers' Guild, of which I was then secretary, and I had the pleasure of driving Cedric and Olive down to Hereford, where the presentation was being made. For Cedric everything was a joy: the countryside, the buildings, the farm fields, trees, cattle, hedgerows. For the entire journey he was held in thrall, and no more so than when I took them into the baronial reception room at Hampton Court Castle, where the awards dinner was being held. I was quite certain neither of them had seen anything like that, and their expressions were childlike, exuding pleasure throughout. It was lovely to see, and you soon come to realise that this almost naive enthusiasm and delight is a characteristic that hallmarks Cedric's personality.

What many of those who follow Cedric's walks across the Bay probably don't realise is that his salary – originally from the Queen, in her capacity as the Duke of Lancaster, but now managed by a Trust – is a mere £15 a year, plus the tenancy of an ageing cottage at Grange. Of course, Cedric has been a fisherman all his life, and still has nets out on the sands, as well as his allotment.

The other facet of Cedric's job, probably not widely understood, is that crossing the Bay isn't simply a question of launching out and heading for Grange, Kents Bank or Humphrey Head, but of finding a safe point at which to cross the River Kent. That in itself is made all the more difficult because the course of the river changes almost daily, and certainly over a period of time, and the point at which it is safe to cross has to be tested by Cedric. He does this on a Friday as a rule, going out with colleagues to place a line of 'brobs', traditionally branches of laurel, to mark out a route, which he then follows for that weekend's walks. But it all has to be repeated a week or so later.

Rarely – but it does happen – no safe way across can be found, and walks have to be cancelled. Disappointment all round, not least for Cedric, who is as much at home in the middle of the Bay as he is in front of a fire. But safety is paramount; remember that if Cedric ever says that the walk is cancelled, that's not a decision he takes lightly, because for him there is no greater joy than bringing pleasure to the thousands who dog his footsteps across those rippling sands. Like any pilot, his task is to get everyone to journey's end.

(Terry Marsh is the author of more than 100 books including many Lake District titles. He is an Hon Life Member of the Outdoor Writers' Guild.)

Getting to know you

Derek & Cynthia Whiting

We are two people in London, who have a magical friendship with two people from Cumbria. Living and working in London compelled a desire for everything that is the English countryside, and so it was that we became members of the Surrey & North Sussex Beagle Hunt. For some forty years we travelled north with many of the members and our beagle hounds to spend two weeks in Cartmel.

For twelve years we stayed in a lovely cottage owned by our friends Judith and John Asher, and it was they who resolved that we should meet Cedric. They could never have known what an auspicious and yet terrible day it was to be. The arrangement was made for the morning of 6th February 2004. It proved to be the morning after the tragic loss of life of the cockle pickers. I felt intrusive. Press and television correspondents and photographers abounded, and Cedric had been assisting throughout the night. Nevertheless, he remembered his appointment and would not allow us to cancel and go home.

We could never have known the pleasure to be shared following that first wretched February morning. The meeting arose out of a common profound interest in carriage driving and out of respect and affection for the Duke of Edinburgh. Cedric had guided Prince Philip cross the Bay. Cynthia and I have had the privilege of meeting him so often as members and officials of the Windsor Park Equestrian Club. He was a competitor and in later years a judge and fellow official.

In 2009 we were to become the Guides (in London) to the Queen's Guide to the Sands. Cedric's autobiography *Sandman* was published in that year and on 9th December he was to be interviewed by Libby Purves on BBC Radio. Cedric and Olive would be coming south, but to use his own words, "We would be lost in London." It was the Asher family who put us on notice and it was such a pleasure to be invited to assist.

I took a copy of *Sandman*, signed by the author, and stood with it on the concourse at Euston station. It was a lovely surprise when one of the first passengers off the train came straight to me: "I can see who you are waiting for. He is on the train." The passenger was the head teacher at the school in Cartmel.

We welcomed Cedric and Olive to London. We took them across to Oxford Street, delivered them first to Broadcasting House and then to St George's Hotel. We settled them both, made tea in their room, orientated them and left. They were to have dinner as guests of the BBC. Next morning we stayed at home to listen to the interview and then returned to the hotel.

Most thrilling of all, Cedric and Olive were then able to see the troopers and horses of the Household Cavalry in Horse Guards Parade. We next entered the museum housed in part of the original stable block. I was so pleased for Cedric and there was no entry fee for either of us – as old soldiers! We viewed through glass partitions the stables and the now dismounted troopers going about their duties. The horses were in their stalls and only the smell was missing.

We ultimately returned to St George's, but the magic continued. The Oxford Street lights had been turned on, and I was able to take our visitors this way en route to Euston station on the top deck of a London bus. It had all been such a pleasure.

This first encounter was but a prelude to more. Cedric and Olive came to London again for a

very special occasion – a Royal Garden Party at Buckingham Palace in June 2010. Cynthia was their escort and resolved to bring them from Euston to Victoria on the London Underground. There are not too many moving escalators near to Guides Farm and Olive was thrilled at the prospect of recapturing her youth. She had ridden escalators in a store in Manchester and was happy to repeat the experience on the Underground.

Lunch was at the Rembrandt Hotel directly opposite the gate to the Royal Mews at Buckingham Palace. Afterwards we were able to see the many guests coming out from the grounds – ladies dressed for the occasion and uniforms in abundance. Then it was into a London taxi and over to Euston so that Cedric and Olive could return to Grange. It had been a wonderful day.

(Cedric comments: "Olive and I met Derek and Cynthia Whiting by chance. They are such lovely people. When chatting with them, they said that if we ever came to London we must not hesitate to get in touch, as they would meet us off the train. This they did. Without them as Tour Guides through London, we would rather have stayed at home.")

Crossing a Wet Sahara

Ron Sands

Over 25 years ago when I was living in the Lake District the AA Publications Department invited me to submit a dozen or so extended paragraphs for their new lavishly illustrated book Secret Britain. Although the commission was essentially for the Lake District area the first paragraph that came to mind for me belonged to the very fringes of Lancashire and Cumbria – crossing the sands of Morecambe Bay at low tide, under the unique guidance of Cedric Robinson.

More than any other walk I have ever done this route figured the largest in my imagination and in my memory – thanks to Cedric's heaven sent gifts of description. At the time I had regularly walked Wainwright's routes on the high fells of Cumbria – including the Shamrock Traverse of Pillar, which I had completed so often that I could walk from Ambleside to Ennerdale, and do that remarkable route over a weekend without recourse to any maps.

But even those fabled walking routes faded into insignificance compared with my memories of crossing the sands with Cedric. On one occasion I was in the company of members of the Outdoor Writers' Guild. Some of these members had walked in all parts of the world. Several had written definitive walking guidebooks to here, there and everywhere. It was a group of men (there were no women back then) who were not easily impressed. But every single one of them was soon under Cedric's spell, and the complimentary letters from them, received the following week, were the most impressively eloquent of any that I have received before or since.

Previous pages: Morecambe Bay has been likened to 'a wet Sahara'. It can be truly evocative, whether it be the ripples of wet sand or simply the reflection of walkers. (Paul Nickson; Ian Hughes)

I think it was after that particular walk that one of the writers quoted Cedric's description of the Bay Walk as 'like crossing a wet Sahara', a description that would crop up again from time to time even in the titles of the articles they and others subsequently wrote. 'The Wet Sahara' – that phrase reminds me today of Cedric's spellbinding way with words, which is such a pleasing accompaniment to his expertise as a Guide across a route that can be fraught with danger and risk as well as portraying indescribable peace and beauty.

In my far off Lake District days I was slightly acquainted with two of Lakeland's best known writers – both of them Cumbrians – Melvyn Bragg and Hunter Davies. They too fell under Cedric's spell. Melvyn went on to write one of his finest novels – The Maid of Buttermere – with an opening chapter set in the Bay with a group of 18th Century travellers. And Hunter became another admirer, thanks to Cedric. Norman Nicholson too can be listed in this respect, describing Cedric's crossings as a tremendous curtain raiser to a tour of the Lakes. Of course all three of these modern writers were treading in William Wordsworth's footsteps and today Cedric captures for us the enthusiasm of such writers.

I often think of Cedric when I re-read Wordsworth's description in his *Guide to the Lakes* where he writes that the crossing of the sands is a prequel to a visit to the Lake District. It is, he claims, 'not only a deed of derring do, but also of a decided proof of taste'.

And this for me is Cedric's greatest attribute – he provides a compelling link with centuries of tales of excitement, of breathtaking beauty and of life-threatening danger. And he introduces a younger generation of trekkers, who will recall the experience for the rest of their lives of what for me is the finest corner of 'Secret Britain'. Thank you Cedric for unlocking those secrets in a way that no other guide could ever match.

(Ron Sands is Cabinet Member for Culture, Lancaster City Council)

Sand Pilot – in every sense of the word

Invisible Flock

Nearly 50 years on he sits in a chair with a roaring fire to one side and Olive opposite, as he recollects with a memory as pinpoint and precise as the clock that ticks away above the mantle. He paints pictures of a childhood dominated by a landscape he has helped to define. He remembers those first walks as if recalling a day not long since past. His mind whizzes back to 1963, for us a year of presidential assassinations, a decade young Queen, of cold wars, iron curtains, the Beatles. For Cedric it is a horizon stretching out before him like the future he is yet to traverse. At the start of this year President John F Kennedy will pledge to place a man on the moon, the silver orb hanging unvisited above the Bay.

Cedric steps off the rocky outcrop towards Hest Bank and beyond, little aware I expect that this walk will become as much a part of him as the bare feet that propel him out, fifty years marked as often as possible with one walk in one direction. On this walk he has accumulated enough sand

Members of Invisible Flock, out in the Bay with Cedric in reflective mood.

miles to carry him around the world nearly twice. By 1967 he will have already strolled back and forth enough times to take him on a straight-line trek from Guides Farm to Canada, yet in reality he has never left the country or been on a plane.

A picture of a young Olive hangs on the wall, as striking as the title 'Miss Leeds' would demand. A half-century on, she sits nearby listening to his stories, having lost none of her beauty. She and the Bay are talked of constantly, the two loves of his life, one calm and concerned and the other treacherous and unpredictable.

He talks of jumbos and dykes, melgraves and mires. He is proud of his royal title, but he is far too polite to boast about his impact on this landscape. He has saved lives, admonished tomfoolery, walked with princes and explorers, and safely escorted thousands upon thousands of legs across the Bay.

The phone is rarely off the hook, burned hot with requests and queries. I imagine only stadiums or grand museums attract more interest than his weekend walks. Seven plus miles and just shy of four hours, crossed so regularly and without a single note of dullness in its repetition.

He is the epitome of an ideal walking companion, friendly, supremely knowledgeable, chatty and self-deprecating. He paints masterful pictures with his words, and tells stories so vivid you can imagine them as if they were events from your own memory. He has a regular chortle that punctuates the conversation, the prowess of a great after-dinner speaker.

People come from miles drawn by the dangerous beauty of the sands, the terrible speed with which they can entrap and ensnare – death doesn't tiptoe here it gallops. He never pretends to have tamed this vast submerged desert but to have read it and re-read it like a favourite book. He studies it like the well-worn face of a friend, notes its telltale signs, its tricks and ticks and sleights of hand, and knows when it has bested him and when he must remain at home with the fire, disappointed that no walkers will witness the joys of the Bay today.

But he knows that soon the rivers will not be so high and the quicksand not so wide and that he will be out again, navigating with a whistle and a stick, a sea of faces in his wake as he traipses through the seasons, ticking back and forth like a metronome across the Bay. He is one of a dwindling number of constants within our fast changing, eroding and in-flux lives, a reassuring presence which ensures that no matter what the world is throwing up all around us, he can be found on a weekend edging from one side to the other. His weekly path is marked like a repeated stitch on the landscape, a sand cloth embroidered with his footprints. He is a pilot in every sense of the word.

The silver orb still hangs above the Bay. It mirrors the landscape below, two wildernesses that talk to one another through the tides. The tract of land between the two coastlines which Cedric inhabits is as alien as the one above and for the last five decades he has made it earthbound, giving us the chance to take giant leaps across this moonscape. I push my boot into the soft watery sand and watch as it inevitably dissolves and think of the astronaut's footprint marked on the moon above, and impressions that will remain forever.

(Invisible Flock are an interactive arts organisation based in Leeds: 'We spent the last year meeting with Cedric and Olive, who were far too generous with their time, Cedric granting us the opportunities to follow him about as he fished his nets, tested the sands and led the cross-Bay walk. He was always gracious to answer a barrage of questions whilst Olive served up numerous cups of tea. In partnership with Live at LICA, Arts Council England and Lancashire County Council, we created an art installation and an audio work to accompany the cross-Bay walk. The piece is called Sand Pilot.')

The hero, of course!

Jennifer Burkinshaw

As Jane Austen might have said, it is a truth universally acknowledged that anyone wanting anything about Morecambe Bay must be in need of Cedric Robinson. Having had the privilege of being guided across the Bay by him twice, it is certain that there is nothing that he does not know about his unique and extensive back garden! To cross with Cedric is to be informed, entertained and, most vitally, to be safe.

Having completed the first draft of my novel *We Took Risks*, about teenagers playing dares on Morecambe Bay, who else would I consult to verify the facts and feasibility of certain situations? Cedric has patiently and carefully read the whole 70,000 words, making corrections and explaining matters to me ranging from tide times to rescues from sinking sands. He even appears in the novel – the hero, of course!

Those of you who have met Cedric will know that he is a man of incredible vitality. In September 2012, even though it was impossible to cross, he took a group of us way out onto the sands in teeming rain and perishing winds: he wouldn't disappoint us when we had come to experience its soundscapes. In his yellow waterproof, the weather really did seem to be water off a duck's back, yet I'm sure Cedric would far rather have been with Olive by a roaring fire. But if Cedric can help you with anything whatsoever with Morecambe Bay, you can be one hundred per cent certain that he will make the time to do so.

Just 'Cedric'

Chris Abram

I have walked the length of the Lancashire coast from Banks, near Southport, where I spent my earliest years, through to Morecambe, where I now live. However, walking across Morecambe Bay for the first time is an experience I will never forget – the sense of distance, the 'Big Blue Sky' experience, the silence, the wading birds and other wildlife. Never did I have any thoughts of how dangerous this Bay could be. As teenagers, we used to jump up and down on the sands off the old Carnforth ironworks slag tips to create as much 'Grannies Custard' as we could before the surface broke. Cycling our bike across the estuary of the River Keer through the soggy sands, we would race the fast incoming tide.

All this was years before I met an amazing man. How was it that when I retired to Carnforth, and began researching the Bay's heritage and beauty to put into my films, I was always pointed towards Cedric Robinson? How does it seem now after all these years that everyone to whom I mention the name always breaks out into a smile and tells me their own heart-warming story of Cedric? There's no need for last names – just 'Cedric', for many do not even know his last name, and fewer his age.

I have needed Cedric's experience to feature in several award-winning films that I have made about Morecambe Bay. There is not much that he doesn't know about this area. Fisherman, farmer, excellent father and husband, he is also a raconteur, a gifted speaker and a highly respected worker for innumerable charities. I have experienced all of these and the one thing that comes to the forefront at all times is that he really is a very kind, caring and nice man. The number of events and activities that he undertakes for no remuneration is outstanding.

I have filmed around Morecambe Bay with Cedric many times. When I can get him to stop talking, it becomes obvious to all that here is a totally dedicated man with over fifty years of unbroken service to ensuring the safety and well-being of those adventurous people who want to walk across the Bay and experience the full majesty of the Lake District.

(Chris Abram has filmed Morecambe Bay Our Heritage, Parts 1 to 3. For details see: www.heritagevideoproductions.co.uk)

The Kent Estuary

Peter Standing

The Arnside and Silverdale Area of Outstanding Natural Beauty may be Britain's second smallest AONB after the Scillies but it packs a tremendous variety of limestone scenery, biodiversity and fascinating history into its 75 square kilometres. Over 3,000 hectares of the AONB are in the tidal zone of the Kent estuary and Cedric's most popular sand crossing from White Creek Bay to Kents Bank traverses this zone. Many others have written about the magical experience of crossing the estuary with Cedric, but even just watching his throng of walkers strung out across the sands from the coastal footpath between Arnside and Jenny Brown's Point is a thrilling spectacle.

In June 2012 I organised an educational event in Arnside with lectures, field trips and an exhibition to celebrate the Kent estuary. We were privileged to have Cedric as our guest of honour and he received a standing ovation after his closing address. The focus of the study day concerned how the Kent Estuary works and provided an insight into the challenges faced by Cedric every time he plans a walk.

Estuaries are transition zones between freshwater rivers and saltwater oceans. Although rapidly changing sea level is the most striking feature noticed by shore-bound observers or those unfortunate enough to venture onto the sands during a rising tide, the Kent estuary experiences fluctuations in not just water quantity and flow but also in salinity and temperature. All these factors affect the erosion and accretion of sand and mud and influence the ecology of the estuary.

Morecambe Bay has the second highest UK tidal range after the Bristol Channel and in 2012 the Kent estuary experienced twelve days with tides exceeding ten metres. It is impossible to measure the amount of seawater that funnels into the estuary during one twelve-hour cycle of a ten-metre tide but it is probably over 300 million cubic metres. This creates an extremely dynamic inter-tidal environment with a giant mixing bowl of sediments and ever-changing channels that demand

The Kent estuary, with Arnside viaduct linking the two shores. (Paul Nickson)

respect from human intruders.

The River Kent drains a catchment area of around 590 square kilometres. The quantity of fresh water entering the estuary is also difficult to measure and estimates have to be projected from six hydrometric gauging stations built well upstream of tidal limits. River flow varies according to rainfall and in high flood conditions that of the Kent can be twenty times greater than mean flow. But under average conditions the Kent, Bela and Gilpin between them deliver perhaps 850,000 cubic metres during a twelve-hour tidal cycle. The accuracy of these estimates is not too important – what is clear is that the fresh water input from the Kent catchment is tiny compared with the salt water input from the Irish Sea. The flow patterns of salt and fresh water are also very different.

On Cedric's walks it is common to pause at White Creek awaiting the optimal crossing time and whist waiting here it is worth inspecting the shingle beach. Most of the pebbles are grey limestone but in amongst them you will find other rocks that have been transported along the present estuary course by the Kent glacier. The ice retreated from this area about 18,000 years ago and the deposits of rocks that remain have been further eroded and moved around by tidal forces. Sediment transfer from the upper part of the Kent catchment continues today. Apart from fresh water, the river

Spectacularly beautiful maps of changes in the Kent channel have been created in a study by Lancaster City Council using aerial photography and satellite imagery. This example shows the changes between Grange (top left) and Silverdale (bottom right). (Aerial data copyright E.A./English Nature)

AERIAL DATA COPYRIGHT E.A./ENGLISH NATURE

Channels, circa 1950
Channels, circa 1974
Channels, early 1960's

Scale 1 : 25000

AERIAL SURVEY 24/10/97

also transports these sediments and nutrients derived from the weathering and erosion of the rocks and soils it passes through.

The Kent is a short river rising at the head of Kentmere at an elevation of 750 metres and reaching the normal high tide limits near Sampool after only 45km. In upper Kentmere the geology consists mainly of tough Borrowdale Volcanics Group rocks, whilst the middle section of the river passes through the more easily eroded Windermere Silurian Group producing more gently rounded hills. Downstream of Kendal the rock is mainly Carboniferous limestone, which is seen between Arnside and White Creek Bay.

So next time you walk the sands with Cedric, remember that you are in a macro-tidal estuary where water flows with great force from both directions and that timing your crossing with an experienced leader is all-important. The sediments below your feet have a precarious existence, forever being built up and pulled down in the tremendously dynamic environment of the Kent estuary. Enjoy yourselves but take care!

(Peter Standing is Events Organiser for the Landscape Trust, a charity that supports the Arnside and Silverdale AONB.)

Autumn Cockling

Peter Cherry

In the autumn of 1982 I was taking photographs for my first book On Morecambe Bay. Guides Farm was like a second home and I regarded the Robinsons as a second family. Ced's daughter Jean was now married to Chris, a farmer's son from Claughton near Lancaster and they were living in the converted attic. Chris was happy to help out around the farm and regularly went out on the sands to help Ced fishing.

I looked out through the living room window of Guides Farm which gave a magnificent view of the Bay on this unusually clear day, from just beyond Jenny Brown's Point round to Holme Island. Olive came in to say hello to me and told Ced that she had just had an order for two bags of cockles but there were none to sell. Ced and Chris agreed to go out on the sands the same day to collect some, and looking at his tide tables, Ced declared that they should leave at two-thirty. I eagerly asked to come along and take some photographs.

We set off for the sands once more, on a crisply cold but sunny afternoon, with Chris and me riding on the trailer. This time however we couldn't use the usual railway crossing so turned instead up the steep hill of Carter Road in first gear, then gently downhill the mile to Kents Bank station. We rumbled down to the glutinous mud of the foreshore, then set course for the cockle beds near the end of Cartmel Wharf, just about as far into the Bay as one can go. Ced laughed as we careered into a steep sided channel. I could clearly see the entire arc of the Bay from Blackpool Tower beyond Fleetwood to Heysham, Morecambe, Warton Crag, Silverdale, Arnside Knott and then round past Grange to Piel Island and the distant silhouette of the massive ship yard cranes of

Barrow - familiar places seen from an unfamiliar and ever-shifting viewpoint.

We headed steadily towards Heysham, passing the grassed limestone outcrop of Humphrey Head, said to be the place where the last wild wolf in England was shot. After another quarter of an hour of brisk progress, Heysham didn't seem as close as I would expect; distances viewed across the Bay are deceptive. Another fifteen minutes passed, then without warning we stopped on an area of sand which at first seemed to be like any other. But Ced knew he had arrived at the cockle beds. We unloaded our apparatus and Ced pointed to tiny brown filaments sprouting from the sands. "Cockles are rank here," he declared. 'Rank' means plentiful in the Flookburgh dialect; also 'whee-at' means small or immature cockles, I learned.

Ced hauled the jumbo across the sand and set to work. This implement, thought to be unique to the Flookburgh fisherfolk, is a wooden plank about one foot by four, attached to a pair of handles at waist height by two metal or wood uprights. The plank is rocked to and fro on the sands to soften them, causing the cockles buried an inch or so below the surface to float upwards into view. The cockles can then be flicked into a net using a three-pronged hand fork called a cramb.

Some Flookburgh men are able to pick up a hundred or more cockles a minute by this method, but on this day Chris used a short handled rake to gather them. Ced energetically rocked the jumbo, pulling it back after every five or six rocks to prepare a strip of sand for Chris to work on. The expression, 'rocking the jumbo', belies the back-breaking effort involved, especially when the sand is relatively dry and hard, as I found when Ced let me have a go. Chris raked the cockles into a riddle and poured them into baskets, then washed and filled the shellfish into plastic sacks.

The sun touched the horizon as the last load of cockles was added to top up the second bag, though it had only just turned five-thirty. "That's enough for one day," beamed Ced, his normally ruddy face appearing even redder in the sun's magenta afterglow. Looking at Ced in the twilight on the lonely Bay, I felt a real affection for this friendly man, with his bright yellow oilskin bound tightly at the waist by a length of string.

Turning around, I discovered a full moon sitting on the hills to the east, as if displaced in perfect opposition to the setting sun. Using an upturned bucket on top of one jumbo handle as a makeshift tripod – Ced's idea – I photographed the moonlit Bay. This was an unforgettable sight. The scene seemed appropriate; without the moon there would be no tide and without the tide's ebb and flow, this unique way of life would not exist.

As purple twilight rapidly gathered itself in around us, a string of orange streetlights could be seen, stretching round the coast road from Heysham to Carnforth. To the north was a tiny cluster of pinpoints, which was Flookburgh, and just east of this, an array of bright points on the Grange hillside. Ced steered for this beacon on the homeward journey, passing Humphrey Head once more, which this time loomed as a menacing black shadow. Soon we thankfully reached the gates of Kents Bank crossing, but had to wait for a cold ten minutes before the keeper emerged.

Olive was relieved when we at last returned, by the light of the moon, after four hours away. She soon gave us a meal of roast chicken and Jean's apple pie, accompanied by last year's home-made damson wine. Thereafter, Ced, Jean and Olive soon fell asleep in front of the flames in the hearth of Guides Farm.

(The author's second book, Cherry's Morecambe Bay, *was published in 2011. See: www.petercherry.com)*

The ancient craft of cockling, showing Cedric 'rocking the jumbo' and son-in-law Chris Jackson emptying the cockles out of a riddle. (Peter Cherry - 2)

11. Walks to raise millions

It was fifty years ago that I was able to make my first cross-Bay walk to Grange from Hest Bank with a small group of walkers led no doubt by Cedric Robinson (in the first year of his appointment as the Guide). Since then I have made many crossings from Arnside to Hest Bank with Cedric, mainly with groups raising money for charity. Up to 600 walkers have made the crossing on many of the walks and thousands of pounds have been raised.

Cedric has always made me welcome and asks me to accompany him at the front to keep the groups in check when crossing the many channels encountered. Each walk is totally different from the previous one on account of the channels and the possibility of shifting sands.
Barry Ayr

In 1982 two ladies decided to 'walk the Bay' for fun. The day before going they asked for sponsor forms, thinking they might as well do some good at the same time. One of their friends had leukaemia and so the Blackpool, Fylde & Wyre Branch of the Leukaemia Research Fund became involved and were the happy recipients of £220, which the ladies raised in just twenty-four hours. This was then a lot of money.

The following year their friend had been admitted to Trinity Hospice in the Fylde, and we were asked if we would organise a walk and divide the money raised between the Fund and the Hospice. It was decided to advertise the first walk by inviting Cedric Robinson to bring his films and tell us about it, which he duly did. The event was a great success, attracting people from all over the Blackpool and Fylde area.

Thus began a very happy association between the two charities and Cedric and Olive Robinson. The walks continued until 2010, when bureaucracy made it impossible for them to be organised as before. In that time we have raised over £100,000, giving each charity over £50,000. We believe that we were the first charities to organise the Bay Walk in this way, but many others followed suit.

The walks gave people a chance to chat to Cedric about his work and what was involved in managing the actual routes across – no easy task and a huge responsibility. He is a character and very knowledgeable about the moods of the Bay. His phone calls to me in January to arrange the date for the coming year always began with a discussion about farming, the weather and what he had been doing – and then finally the date!
Doreen Sykes and Marjorie Wilkinson

Opposite: top: The first walk to be led by Cedric following his appointment as the Queen's Guide in November 1963. Then only 30, he is seen on the right of this photograph.

Bottom: One of the early walks about 1964 heads across the Bay with a much younger Cedric and Olive at the front. Compared with today, the numbers taking part were tiny.

Contrasts on a glorious walk: Striding out with a purpose; leaving behind hundreds of footprints; keeping up with Cedric in deeper water; and pausing to take a photograph. This event was organised by the University of Central Lancashire in support of its Harris Bursary Fund and the LEP Lifesaver Appeal. (Neil Stanley – 4)

It was several years ago that I first experienced the wonders of being guided across Morecambe Bay by Cedric Robinson. On the first walk we joined a large national charity, parking at Grange over Sands and travelling by coach to the start at Arnside. Acting on advice, we were well prepared with shorts, old trainers, sun cream – oh, yes, the sun does shine in the Lakes – and thankfully water, coffee and sandwiches.

What an experience as some 400 of us excitedly got out of the coaches at Arnside. Cedric was waiting with a big smile, jeans rolled up, a whistle and a stick. Off we went across the sands – old, young, babes in arms and many very happy dogs of all shapes and sizes. How very British we looked as if we were following the pied piper with his whistle.

The sands started out dry and flat but this changed to damp and rippled from the ebbing tide as it receded from the Bay. We soon realised as we waded through the remaining channels that not all the water had gone. Hence the need for shorts – and many chose to go barefoot. How the dogs and the children loved it. There was much mirthful chatter among the walkers and it was certainly fun.

On reaching Kents Bank there was a feeling of elation and achievement as we looked back towards Arnside and saw the large swathe of the Bay we had just walked across. Our ageing knees had served us well on the eight to nine miles, but they didn't like the ups and downs and hard pavements to reach Grange. Oh what a great feeling as we sat on the boot edge of our cars, washing our aching feet in the still warm soapy water we had brought from home. Then a change of shorts hidden behind towels – it brought back memories of childhood and those family beach holidays.

The feeling of well-being and camaraderie between all the participants is something only those who have taken part can appreciate, especially as we realise how much we have raised for charity.

Being inspired by Cedric, I decided to organise a walk across Morecambe Bay on behalf of the charity with which I am involved – the Friends of Chernobyl Children (South Lakes). We bring to the UK disadvantaged children from very poor regions of Belarus, which was seriously affected by the Chernobyl nuclear disaster, and provide them with four weeks' recuperative holiday.

On contacting Cedric to book a date for the walk, he could not have been more helpful and gave me a massive amount of advice. We walked on a lovely sunny day in September 2012 with friends and family. All enjoyed the day and £2,500 was raised for our charity. Cedric has also offered to take the children out into the Bay on Sandpiper to go fishing. How lucky they are – I am wishing it were for adults!

I cannot say how much money all the walks led by Cedric have raised – it must over the years go into millions of pounds. I can only say what a very, very special human being he is.
Susan Bain

It was June 1992 and I was embarking on a new chapter in my working life as I joined the Lancashire-based charity, Galloway's Society for the Blind. One of my first postings was as a development officer in Morecambe to increase the range of support and services to the growing number of more than 1,500 people suffering with sight problems.

One summer afternoon, sitting on a rusty old bench next to our Sight Advisory Centre, I thought we ought to make this a haven for our members and a sensory garden was the top of the wish list.

The only problem was how to raise funds for such an expensive project. Volunteers had done some wonderful drawings and even created a scale model – I just knew we had to get the job done!

"Do the Morecambe Bay Walk" was the cry from members, and so I plucked up the courage to ring the Queen's Guide to the Sands. I was surprised when I spoke to a lovely warm and friendly lady who turned out to be Olive, the wonderful wife of Cedric. She invited me to visit and tell them of our plans. The rest you could say is history, as the sensory garden was duly created, but there is so much more to tell. From Galloway's perspective the walk has become the single most successful event in the charity's 146-year history in terms of both number of walkers and funds raised.

The charity remains indebted to the generous support from Cedric and Olive, who are indirectly responsible for making such a difference to the lives of thousands of blind and visually impaired people. It seems such a cliché to say it, but we truly couldn't do what we do without the help of Cedric – and the walks and sponsors who have changed the lives of so many people.

We have so many special memories, from the joy of a wedding on the sands to the tragedy of the last cockler being found as we obliviously walked a number of miles away. There have been the safe crossings of the great and the good, who mingled among the hundreds of walkers that join us every year. What has also been rewarding is the numbers of blind and visually impaired people that have taken part and whose sense of achievement has been immense.

2013 is a very special year for Cedric, and also for Galloway's as we celebrate our thirtieth walk. We again hope to raise funds to help us continue making a difference. From a personal view, I wish to thank Cedric and Olive for their kindness in welcoming me and allowing me to share a small insight into their unique lives.

Kevin Lonergan

I can scarcely believe it is fourteen years since the first sponsored walk across Morecambe Bay in aid of Derian House Children's Hospice, and fifteen years since I first met Cedric at Guides Farm on a gloriously sunny July afternoon. I'm not sure what I was expecting as I drove up across Lancashire to Grange and on down Carter Lane to the farm. What I found was a delightfully unassuming, quietly spoken man, with a calm air of assurance and a great sense of humour, who knows the Kent Sands like his own back yard – which essentially is exactly what they are!

That afternoon, sitting in Cedric's garden in the sunshine, listening to his wonderful stories about the Bay and supplied with tea and cakes by Olive, was one of the most entertaining and fascinating I have ever spent. It was with great reluctance that I finally took my leave of them.

Twelve months later I was back, with 200 Derian House supporters, trekking across the sand, negotiating the channels and just occasionally experiencing the thrill of real quicksand. We were all on a mission to raise as much money as possible for the hospice, with Cedric, staff in hand, leading us forward like some latter day Moses!

Since that very first walk in 1999, nearly 2,000 people have crossed the Bay for Derian House and raised an amazing £95,000. None of this would have been possible without Cedric's generosity and expertise. Without doubt we, and many other charities, would be much the poorer, both financially and experientially, without him.

So on behalf of myself and everyone at Derian House Children's Hospice in Chorley, I would like

Wet pants and moments of unease are part of the course when wading through the deeper water. (Susie Poppitt)

to say an immense thank you and wish Cedric a wonderful and happy 50th anniversary year in his role as Queen's Guide to the Sands of Morecambe Bay.
Susie Poppitt

The anticipation and excitement before a walk with Cedric is truly fantastic – and the sense of achievement at the end equally so! Walking on wet sand with 300 people sounds exceedingly unappealing, but it is truly fun. Everybody is happy, but also a little worried about the rivers in the middle. After the wading is achieved – sometimes with wet pants! – there is then the slimy mud. Oh dear!

Never mind – we get there, hopping from tussock to tussock of grass at the end. Then a smiling Olive hands out certificates to prove we've done it!

Over a number of years, Shipley Support Group have raised over £50,000 for Manorlands Sue Ryder Hospice at Oxenhope through the Morecambe Bay Walk. Thank you Cedric – we could not have done it without you and your splendid helpers. It really is a great experience – rain or shine!
Amy Booth

I first met Cedric when I was involved in organising a walk in aid of Marie Curie Cancer Care. I remember the first group getting to the end of the walk, where I was greeted with the words, "It was brilliant – you definitely couldn't do that without a Guide."

I have now organised twelve charity cross-Bay walks and still people gather at the start at Arnside and comment on Kents Bank not being that far away. They simply don't understand until they complete it that Cedric has to guide them towards Morecambe to avoid quicksand and high water before heading across the Bay.

After the initial walk in 2001, once word spread that it was going to be made into an annual fund-raiser for the charity, we had many people repeat it on a yearly basis, along with new ones who had heard such good reports. Eventually numbers got so high that in one year I had to arrange a second walk with Cedric.

In 2012 I organised my first one for the North West Air Ambulance, which raised more than £10,000 – enough to cover the cost of four rescues – so it goes without saying that it will now become an annual event. Walkers said it was the most 'daring and scariest' walk they had done, as at times they were up to their waist in water. But they added that it was a brilliant challenge.

Cedric's skill has not only raised in excess of £250,000 for my two charities, but it has also put the cross-Bay walk and the area on the map and given many, many people a brilliant day out.
Zoe Casson

Paying rapt attention at the start of a walk, when Cedric issues essential instructions and also finds time to chat to participants. (Ian Hughes)

Thirteen times I've experienced the expectancy around the Arnside foreshore as people gather for the Morecambe Bay Walk. Suddenly people start nudging each other and whispering, "That's him, that's Cedric", as a weather-beaten man, stout stick in hand, appears from nowhere and walks up the street. Like the children of Hamelin following the pied piper, everyone falls in and follows him – the one and only Cedric. We are all perfectly happy to trust ourselves to his guidance.

Cedric stops and chats to people, letting the stragglers catch up, telling us stories of the sands, like the two lads on quad bikes who got into the quicksand and phoned their dad to come in his 4x4 to pull them out. Cedric stopped him and managed to get a rope from his tractor round one of the bikes before it disappeared totally, and they pulled it clear. He then said, "The other will come up in three or four weeks when the sea's had enough of it!" Everyone who takes part has a story to tell and there is always a buzz on the coach on the way home – then silence descends as they fall asleep with their memories.

Cedric has enabled my group to raise over £120,000 for the Christie Hospital in Manchester alone. How many millions he's helped other charities to raise I don't know, but it's much appreciated and probably unique. As our supporters get off the coach, many say to me: "I've always wanted to do the walk – thank you." No, thank YOU, Cedric.
Janice Moss

Cedric has been helping me organise walks across the sands of Morecambe Bay since I first entered into charity work over fifteen years ago, and more recently with two walks a year in my role as fundraising officer for the Meningitis Trust. I estimate that the amount raised for the two charities has been in the region of £25,000, which is incredible.

Cedric is always willing to share his passion and knowledge of the Bay with all our walkers, which makes this very special for them. He is friendly, thoughtful and utterly reliable – and never fails to support our charity each year. Even when the weather has been bad and we have not been able to walk, he has always been quick to re-arrange another date for us, understanding the importance of the vital funds we need.

Our supporters come from far and wide just to walk alongside Cedric. They love the open space and fresh air. The fact that they are walking somewhere quite dangerous and could not do this without Cedric's expert knowledge makes the walk that more enjoyable for people. The children love the tractor when it comes out into the Bay to meet them, just as some of them might be struggling and making it rather hard for their parents.

Christine Hughes

Sitting down to write a fitting tribute to someone like Cedric Robinson is daunting to say the least. He is a legend, not only in Morecambe Bay and its adjoining counties, but throughout the UK and even beyond. I am lucky enough to live on the Bay and I am also privileged to run the Rosemere Cancer Foundation, a local charity that raises money for additional facilities for cancer patients treated in Lancashire and South Cumbria. Events such as the Cross Bay Walk are vital to Rosemere's income, and in 2012 alone 304 supporters accompanied Cedric across the sands on a glorious August Sunday to raise over £8,000 in sponsorship.

Throughout the summer Cedric selflessly gives of his time and expertise to help charities like Rosemere raise much needed funds, and in the process he allows the public a unique view of Morecambe Bay. I can't believe he's 80 years young as he doesn't look a day older than when I first met him over a decade ago. On behalf of all those who have enjoyed his company on the Bay over the years, and all those who have benefited from the thousands and thousands he has helped to raise for good causes, I give heartfelt thanks.

Sue Thompson

Thanks have also been received from:
Alice Atkinson (Bolton Hospice)
Helen Duxbury (Cumbria Wildlife Trust)
Judith Read (Morecambe Bay Hospitals Charity)
Peter Rimmer (Arthritis Research UK and Bay Search & Rescue)
Stephen Tongue (British Red Cross – Northern Counties)

12. Horses across the Bay

As children my sister and I used to visit Morecambe with our parents and would always ask to ride the beach ponies. Although not able to own a pony, we were and to a certain extent still are 'horse mad'. It had for many years been a dream of mine to ride across Morecambe Bay on a horse.

Eleven years ago, on a most beautiful August day, I walked across the Bay with Cedric – accompanied by some 500 other walkers – all in aid of charity. It was during this walk that I was able to ask him if he would take a group of horse riders across. To my utter delight he said he would – and as the saying goes 'the rest is history'.

We have been across and back every year since then, sometimes even being able to ride across twice in one year. Once we had twenty-five riders, and photographers from two newspapers along with us – and articles were subsequently published.

Every time we take to the sands with our horses we have absolute faith in Cedric, along with John and Mike, to guide us across and back again in complete safety. He, and only he, is the person we trust with our lives and the lives of our precious horses.

My lovely Spanish horse, Flamenca, was the one I rode across on many occasions, galloping across the river, and I am sure that she enjoyed the experience as much as I did. On one occasion there was no stopping her – and her enthusiasm was more than I had anticipated. But control was soon re-established and we all returned safely.

Thanks to Cedric and his team, many horse riders have had the chance to experience the absolute joy and exhilaration of riding across one of the most beautiful places known to man.

Phyllis Capstick

In 2003 I was approached by Phyllis Capstick when she was trying to arrange for a group of bridleway riders to cross Morecambe Bay. She asked if I would be prepared to transport Cedric Robinson to lead the group on my carriage with Spirit, my grey cob. At first I said it was a risky job, but then replied, "Well, if he was trusted to take the Duke of Edinburgh on the same route in the 1980s, he is good enough for me."

What an opportunity and privilege to take Cedric on what turned out to be many more trips, now totalling eleven. It has been one of life's great experiences to meet a man such as Cedric. I would say he is a legend, a man with great knowledge of the sands thank goodness, and he has a great sense of humour. For example, on one crossing he said, "Make for the white-fronted house in the distance." There must have been thirty to forty white-fronted houses!

Thank you Cedric for the pleasure of sharing the beauty of the sands with you.

Bryan H. Procter

Horse riders go out into the Bay in all weathers – and are not afraid of the challenge of descending into a deep channel.
(Bryan Capstick – 2)

Setting off on a cross-Bay ride creates a feeling of mounting excitement. This procession is leaving Kents Bank station. (Bryan Capstick)

As soon as Phyllis phones up to inform us that there is a cross-Bay ride the adrenalin rises in eager anticipation to the appointed day. One never knows how the day will turn out. Assembling at Kents Bank or more recently on the shore at Humphrey Head, the feeling of excitement probably spreads to the horses, never mind the riders!

When all are assembled, mounted and ready for the off, Cedric gives us our instructions. He travels in front of the horses on a trap, driven by his friend, pulled by an obliging grey dappled cob. The clear instructions are that the riders are to follow the trap, keeping inside the wheel tracks to ensure that the terrain ridden on is firm. All the horses begin to juxtaposition in their excitement to get to the front. Riders too no doubt feel the same anticipation of impending fun.

Some horses attempt to go outside the allocated path, but soon realise that this is not only frowned upon but also unwise as some have found out to their peril. There is also a tractor escorting the group, bringing any accompanying person who is not riding, plus other interested people. Cedric often checks that all are in control and happy, with one or two stops to ensure the group keeps together.

It is hard to believe when one looks at the map, or crosses the Bay on the train, that there is a particular place somewhere in the middle where one cannot see land on either side. We have done it in fearsomely wet conditions where we could have been on the moon for what could we see (or in our case could not see!). However, the reassurance of the pony and trap guiding us is sufficient for us to continue on to the other side.

When we come to halt a short distance from the opposite coast, a little way south of Arnside, there is sometimes a moment to reflect on how we have got there. For anyone who has not ridden the Bay before, they probably do not know what is now in store. When everyone is ready, remounting if necessary, and well refreshed, Cedric informs us that we can return 'at our own speed'.

This means that anyone who wishes can go 'hell-for-leather', including through the water channels, so long as everyone remains inside the wheel tracks of the trap and inside the laurel markers in the channels. Well, possible pandemonium breaks out. The speed merchants set off at a gallop, the more sedate at a canter. How long this can be maintained by the various horses depends on either their fitness or the determination of the riders! It must be nearly eight miles back, so there is no way a horse can keep up such a speed for all that distance. There is time to get one's breath back, as Phyllis riding her Andalucian high-stepping chestnut leads the chase (as this is what is has become!).

It is certainly an adrenalin rush as we set off at high speed on the return journey. Such speed and fun is rarely experienced outside of hunting and there is no doubt that both horses and riders return full of appreciation for the opportunity to have had such a brilliant and exhilarating day. Always one for the memory bank!

When we get back to dry land, it is thanks to Phyllis for organising and inviting us to participate. Thanks also to Cedric for trusting us to behave and return safely. Long may these rides continue across the Bay!

June Chapman

The Morecambe Bay ride is probably one of the most exciting experiences I have ever had. I had walked across the Bay on several occasions, but when I heard from Phyllis about the proposed ride, I decided with some trepidation that I wanted to try. My trusty steed was my Fell, Townend Banner, who was about 25 years old at the time, who was not particularly noted for being brave through water and whose preferred gait was a steady plod with the occasional trot. 'Slow and steady' was Banner's motto, though he would go all day in that manner. So what – let's give it a go!

It was a glorious day and twenty or so riders set off on the adventure. I was quite proud because Banner went across the level crossing at Kent's Bank with no fuss but then came the first dyke with a narrow stream of shallow water in the bottom. "No way," said Banner. It was slippery, muddy and wet! All the others got across and Banner watched their antics. I was thinking that was it when, with a sudden leap (well, hop really because Banner did not do leaps either), we were across and in a flurry to catch up. He was not being left either!

From then on he was in his seventh heaven – and so was I. That day was a wonderful ride. Banner was a different pony out there, in a good way. He walked, trotted and even cantered with the best of them, the most exhilarating part being the gallop through the water in the wide channel, part way across, not deep but quite hard work for Banner's little legs. He was like a rocking horse, lifting his legs out of the water with each stride – I shall never forget the effort he put in to do it!

We had an interesting experience on the way back. Cedric, who was very carefully leading and guiding the whole ride, told the riders that they could now safely make their own way back but that they must follow a wide curve to avoid the quicksand. The bulk of the riders were off at a good gallop. I thought I would take it easy and follow at a quieter pace with Banner. He had done his effort.

I held him back for a few moments and then off we set. But Banner did not want to know the wide curve – nor the 'quiet'. Direct was his chosen route and, a bit scarily, I struggled to pull him around a bit. However, thankfully, we did not disappear and safely arrived at Kents Bank triumphant though with a soaked mobile phone (strapped to my leg unfortunately and never to work again). Just brilliant!

I did that ride with Banner on two more occasions but, when he got to 28 years old, I was a bit worried that he would push himself too hard in the excitement and have a heart attack out there! So we called it a day. We did return for the filming of 'Countryfile', really not intending to go out on the Bay again and just wanting to see the fun. Banner and I stayed on dry ground and were rewarded by meeting up with Matt Baker on the shore eating barbecued lamb from the Holker Estate. We had a chat and a photo call (!) and I think that was a very satisfying and memorable end to our adventures across Morecambe Bay.

Thank you to Phyllis for even thinking about such an adventure, thank you to Cedric for carefully guiding us across that dangerous but spectacular landscape on so many occasions, and a special thank you to Banner for giving me the confidence to share in such a wonderful experience.
Barbara Hartley

Being lucky enough to work around the Bay, I see it from every angle in all weathers. One day I might be in Morecambe looking across to Ulverston, admiring a sudden unexpected shaft of sunshine lighting up the white lighthouse, the next I could be stealing a walk up Hampsfell at lunchtime, stopping to gaze at the amazing panoramic view. So, when the chance came to ride across the Bay, during the year I turned 50, it seemed too good an opportunity to miss. It would be a small achievement for me and my black and white cob to mark a significant birthday year.

I had had Jake since he was nine months old. I started learning to ride when I was just seven and was one of those dreadful children whose constant question "Daddy can I have a pony?" must have driven my parents mad. The answer was always a definite "NO"! So, when I finally got my gangly beast from the local hunt kennel, for the princely sum of £200, it really was a dream come true. I was 37, so it had been a long wait.

Several friends declined the offer to join us. Crossing Morecambe Bay with its fearsome reputation is not everyone's idea of a good time. But I had walked across several years before, so I knew a bit about Cedric and his team and had complete confidence in the safety and planning.

The ride was to be on the 7th June 2010 leaving from Humphrey Head, crossing to Arnside and of course back. The weather was perfect. Not too hot but bright sunshine and clear, sharp visibility. I think we were due to leave at 1.30 and everyone was tacked up and looking ready for the off. Cedric had arrived and was pottering about chatting to people and admiring the horses. I hadn't

Horse riders were requested by 'Countryfile' for a programme about Cedric crossing the Bay. Barbara Hartley was able to join Matt Baker in a 'photo call'.

realised he was a horse person, but thinking about it he must be otherwise why would he be willing to lead such a unique ride?

Jake held his head held high and with his fluffed fetlocks fluttering. I had imagined that we'd walk quite a lot of the way and maybe raise the odd canter when it was very safe: little did I know. Rather suddenly we were round the head towards the open sands. Jake was full of busy and up for the challenge. Unfortunately, he was so up for the challenge that he decided to stop and deposit a big pooh on the bank of the first channel we had to cross – this gave one of the horses behind time to think and decide that she didn't fancy crossing a ditch. She leapt and 'pronked' and cavorted giving her rider a rare old battle. Several riders went back to help and persuade whilst I watched from a distance feeling as if it was my fault. It made me realise what a wuss I really am. There is no way I'd want to sit on top of an elegant, feisty beast with back legs like coiled springs. Give me my 15.2 chunky cob any day.

Finally, with Cedric seated in a trap behind a smart little pony and the Sandpiper (a tractor towing a jingly trailer with seats) out in front, we headed for the open sands. With strict instructions to stay behind the pony and trap we progressed at a spanking pace. None of your ploddy walking – a smart, bouncy trot all the way. It was great fun and amazing to be out on the sands looking back at the headland and across the Bay to Arnside. The perfect weather gave us the most breathtaking views and the shimmer of sun on wet sand was magical. Jake was having a rare old time; he'd decided that company was a good thing but that he rather liked to be near the front!

We were fast approaching the River Kent as it flowed out into the Bay and Cedric stopped to

The fact that most horses cope well with quite deep water out in the Bay adds to the feeling of exhilaration. (Bryan Capstick)

explain how to cross it safely. He had placed laurel branches at either end of the safe crossing stretch and told us to spread out and not follow one another. The sand in the channel would get poached up and heavy very quickly and could make horses following loose their footing. The water was quite deep – bearing in mind Jake was 15.2 and I still managed to get wet feet.

The noise was terrific, twenty-plus horses all striding through the deep water. It felt like a bit part in an old Western – all marching forward watching for the Injuns to appear. One person did take a dip as her horse decided it would rather follow its chum and, sure enough, it stumbled and pitched the poor woman into the water. She was very cool about it though and scrambled back on smartly, none the worse for a brief swim.

We arrived on the Arnside side of the Bay in good order to be met by representatives of the North Lancashire Bridleways Society offering us orange squash and custard cream biscuits. Not perhaps a snack of choice, but extremely welcome and the old adage about food tasting better in the open air held true – the best custard cream biscuits since I was the biscuit monitor at primary school.

Jake, not being partial to custard creams, stood still and stretched his neck in a rather yoga-like movement. He seemed to be dozing and several people doubted that he'd raise a trot on the homeward straight. However, after a few minutes break and the thought that time and tide wait for no man (or horse), we were headed back across the sands. Shortly after re-crossing the Kent, Cedric again pulled us up with an instruction.

"If you want to gallop," he said, "Follow the hoof prints."

There was a chap leading the ride from horseback who began to say, "Once this mare goes, she's …." And he was off, tearing across the sands along with a few other big, beautiful beasts in pursuit. I tried to hold Jake back, bearing in mind the yoga and apparent fatigue during the break, but he was having none of it. We jiggled and pranced until four other horses decided to gallop and shot past us and I decided to give up and let him go.

With a rather unladylike "Oh bugger it – we'll go", we overtook the pony and trap and Jake had his first proper gallop. He was terrific, and just kept going. I did try to steady him several times but he really wanted to gallop. It was so exhilarating. From where I was it felt like we were flying. Probably, from the Sandpiper we just looked like a chunky cob topped off with a flappy old rider – but what the heck. It was fantastic!

When I looked up to see where the others had got to, I was amazed to see several tiny horses, way, way in the distance. For a moment I thought someone must be exercising racehorses, but they were actually the beauties from our ride that had taken off first. I wished I had my camera, not that I'd have used it, too busy hanging on, but the silhouettes of the horses against the sparkling sand is an image that will stay with me forever.

We ended the ride jogging along behind the Sandpiper, chatting with Cedric and company about big-hearted, lovely cobs like Jake and appreciating what a superb day it had been. Certainly the biggest highlight of my equine career.

(Very sadly, I lost Jake to colic early in 2012. He had struggled with intermittent bouts since I got him, but they had got steadily worse during the early months of this year. He was just 15. He is irreplaceable and I was very, very lucky that he was mine.)
Sheena Robertson

(Thanks also to Naylor Beverley, Elaine Dawson, June Eastham, Glenda Griffin, Anna Howarth, Bryan Melia, Patricia Oliver and Kathryn Richardson for submitting details of their memorable rides across Morecambe Bay.)

****

Quite different to those who ride across the Bay on horseback are members of the Ribble Valley Driving Club. They have a spectacular annual event when members drive across in horse-drawn carriages. The organiser is Ted Smith, a retired farmer. Cedric comments: "His horse is special. A retired trotting horse, Tom can go like the wind." Sharon Smith, who is Ted's daughter, writes below about the thrill of the drive. Her experiences are followed by those of two other members of the Club.

We set off from Kents Bank one lovely sunny July morning. I was driving my cob Billy with my granddad as co-pilot. We headed to Chapel Island and we all got in line behind my dad driving Tom with Cedric on board. All the horses were pulling and trying to race but we kept in line.

Once we reached the first dyke, Cedric waved us all round and we set off at full speed through the dyke. It was like the charge of the light brigade. The water was up around our feet as the horses charged on. We were soaked to the skin but didn't mind – the thrill spurred us on.

When we reached Chapel Island we stopped to rest our horses and listen to some of Cedric's tales. He also showed us how to tread the sand for cockles. We then followed his instructions and headed back to shore. We were covered from head to toe in sand, but we were buzzing and didn't mind. You couldn't wipe the smile off my granddad's face and for that I'll always be grateful to Cedric.

Sharon Smith

Ribble Valley Driving Club has had the privilege of driving across Morecambe Bay many times during the last twenty-three years, just as did the coaches of old. This is entirely due to the expertise of Cedric Robinson, without whom you wouldn't dare to venture.

The drive itself is an exhilarating, exciting, sometimes a little frightening experience, not one for the faint-hearted but definitely not one to be missed! On our first venture in 1989 we went from Arnside to Kents Bank, but now we usually drive out from Kents Bank to the white cliffs – a distance of about seven miles. The precise route taken varies each time, depending on the weather, tides and sand conditions. We are under strict instructions not to deviate in any way from the marked path as the sands are so dangerous!

Cedric sits up on the first carriage with Ted Smith, the Club's President, whose faithful trotter Tom always sets a cracking pace. The rest of us are in a line behind, in all manner of exercise buggies and vehicles. You wouldn't risk a vintage or expensive carriage as the salt and sand doesn't do them any good. The vehicles are pulled by coloured cobs, native ponies, Arabs and equines of every size and shape.

We do sometimes have adventures. On my first crossing the carriage directly in front of me tipped over descending a steep gully, but everyone helped unyoke the horse, upright the carriage and pick up the driver. All concerned were unhurt and bravely carried on.

On another occasion as we crossed the river, a picnic basket was washed off the back of a carriage due to the force of the water. Very bravely, one of Cedric's helpers along with one of our members rode back into the water and managed to retrieve it – with no harm done!

During the crossing we stop to give the horses a breather and Cedric keeps us entertained with tales of going cockling in his youth, using horse-drawn carts. He tells of horses having to swim to beat the tide and has lots of other enthralling stories. His knowledge of the Bay is phenomenal. One year while we were resting, he came round to everyone and advised us to keep gently walking the horses round and not let them stand still. The sand was creeping up their hooves, even though we had only been standing for a few moments.

On the way back we are instructed to get a move on, as the tide waits for no man, so away we go. Sometimes if the river is deep some of the smaller ponies have to swim, which they enjoy immensely. They all rise to the occasion, galloping in the wet sand, and covering us and themselves with it in the process.

Crossing Morecambe Bay is only made possible due to the skill and experience of Cedric – a very special person, one of life's great characters and a real gentleman.

Carol Parker

The annual crossing of the Bay by members of the Ribble Valley Driving Club is a truly spectacular sight. (Paul Nickson)

Much clinking and stamping, excited children and anxious faces, but a general hushed air clung to the assembled crowd at Kents Bank on that warm misty morning. Booked a full year in advance, the ride was still at the mercy of tides, storms and nature's full force.

Cedric scrambled into the lead carriage. Everyone listened earnestly as he issued strict instructions not to be disobeyed on pain of disappearing forever in the shifting quicksand of the infamous Morecambe Bay. Many an unwary traveller, including horses and carriages, has been claimed over the centuries.

As we set off in single file across the sands it was hard to hold back the horses, as they got caught up in the excitement and felt the sand beneath their hooves. Several times we had to swerve from the track to avoid hitting the carriage ahead, and my stomach lurched as the hungry sands beckoned. Ten horses and carriages snaked across the vast Bay and provided a spectacular sight

The event is organised by Ted Smith, seen here with Cedric along with Tom, the spirited trotting horse. (Paul Nickson)

for those still on firm ground.

As we approached the first river we were issued with further instructions. Everyone to cross together, abreast at trot, keep moving – or else! This was only eighteen inches deep and fun. The next river was the same procedure but much deeper. At the third river we were waist deep, even sat within the carriage! We finally arrived at White Creek, our destination, and were able to rest the horses without them and the carriages starting to sink.

A short break and then back across the Bay – much faster this time, and much wetter. Everyone arrived back at Kents Bank wet, muddy and totally exhilarated. It was most definitely the experience of a lifetime.

Pauline Sheridan

Afterword

Patrick Kelly

(Archbishop of Liverpool)

I was born at the house on the corner near the Winter Gardens Theatre, Morecambe. The late Dick Quick gave me an oil painting with a harvest moon casting strange light on the Bay but showing that house, before the Winter Gardens was built. I grew up with Morecambe Bay just there. We learnt to appreciate the Bay in all its moods. Waves breaking over the stone jetty or the whole Bay turned blood red at sunset on 29 June 1965. Winter days when the Lakeland hills, covered in snow were reflected on a still sea. Early spring mornings on the bicycle with the westerly wind behind me going to Saint Mary's for Mass at 6.45.

I often think it was the magic of those early mornings during Lent that sowed the seed of offering to become a priest. That decision meant I set out on a road to bring me to be Liverpool's Archbishop. The family of the first Archbishop, Thomas Whiteside, lived on Saint George's Quay, Lancaster.

I always enjoyed going out on the boats which offered sails to holidaymakers. I liked the yachts, when you all had to duck as the sail was swung across to return home: I wonder what Health & Safety would say today? Best of all the longer sails to Heysham or even across the Bay to Humphrey Head.

And the beauty of the Bay is part of the unique character of the Parish Church in Heysham. I rejoice to see, as I sit at my desk, besides a watercolour by Bernard Atherton of the entrance to the Church of the Holy Sepulchre in Jerusalem, a second watercolour by David Walsby of the Heysham Parish Church as it looks in autumn. And close by there is a Hargreaves water colour of fishing boats with the stone jetty as it was; the number on one of the boats is LR 171 and I think the other is LR6 5. Heysham Parish Church is the only one I know where you walk down to it, step down into the porch then step down into the main body; I think I would fight for a seat near the windows on the left so that looking out across the Bay would be a welcome alternative to listening to the sermons.

Then up on to the headland to the ruins of the older chapel, the question of Saint Patrick and the recent excavations determining ancient routes out across the Bay. But now that same place has the background hum from the power station. I may not tread arrogantly on issues of the need for electricity and employment, the danger of the Nimby attitude – Not In My Back Yard – but I still wonder: is it the most appropriate setting for this development?

And that question was brought home to me even more vividly when in 2011 I found myself convalescing at Boarbank Hall, above Flookburgh, after a hip replacement and day by day rejoiced to see the Bay. But from that side it is dominated to no small extent by the power station out towards the Irish Sea. The fact I could walk and see the Bay all the time, with Humphrey Head from a very different perspective, hastened my recovery and the success of the physiotherapy.

And so to the cross-Bay walk: I wish I could have made them more often, but most of my priestly life has been spent some distance from Morecambe and my diary is not exactly in my control. But I choose to mention one in particular. Several times I have been sponsored on walks, with others, to raise money for the movement Right to Life, which seeks to respect life from its earliest beginnings to its end enfolding every life with respect, dignity and love.

The most important one for me was shortly after the tragedy of the cockle pickers. The Bay was not in its gentlest mood as Cedric led us on safely and firmly on our way; swiftly flowing abundant water in the river, squally showers, staggering contrast of light up the Lakeland valleys and much mud to greet us as we came back ashore. But it felt like a reclaiming of the Bay as a place of life in abundance, wonder, respect, awe, fun and joy. That determination was reflected in the Civic Service held in Saint Peter's Cathedral, Lancaster, at that time.

That wonder has been shared by Cedric with thousands. It is a privilege indeed to be associated with this publication to mark Cedric's 50 years as Queen's Guide to the Sands of Morecambe Bay and his 80th birthday. When I reach my 75th birthday in 2013 I must follow the Roman Catholic way and offer my resignation as Archbishop to the Pope. I will be doing my best to make sure that when the Leaving of Liverpool is for me I may find a home close to the Bay.

The last rays of the setting sun highlight glorious Morecambe Bay – a wonder that Cedric has shared with thousands. (Paul Nickson)

Subscribers

Anthony Alston Addison

Janian Aldridge

Alec

Liz Amos

Ann

John Armitage

Derek Arnold

Roger & Fran Arnold

John & Judy Asher

John Alan Ashworth

Mary Attwood

John Richard Bailey

K G Bamford

Barbara

Mary & John Barber

June Barnard

Lorna Barnes

Olga Batty Edwards

N N Beach

Mary Beetham

Richard Beetham

Michael Bell

John Bennett

David N Binns

Andrew J Binns

Roy Birch

Olive & Graham Boulter

Margaret Bowe

Mary Bowford

John Richard Bradley

John Briggs

Cathy Briggs

Ian Brizell

Richard H Broad

Jill Brotherton

Josephine Burrows

David Butterell

Richard Callard

Mike Carter

Barbara Cartlidge

Glenn Chapman

Phil Clayton

Sandra D Collins

Anne Collins

Jill Connors

Nigel Cowell

Richard Crabtree

Richard Cragg

Dorothy Angela Cragg

Cedric Crawford

Nick Cripps

Ron Crofts

Graham Cross GLA

Joan Curphey

Ruth Mary Curwen-Walker

Margaret P Dailey

Tony Daltry

Christopher Darvill

John M Dennis

Rachel Maria Drazek

Dave Drury

Elizabeth Duxbury

Patricia Eccles

Edward

Ann, John & Rose Epps

John Raymond Fishwick

Geoffrey Forbes

Ben Forshaw

Pamela Gee

Geoff & Catherine

Ethel Glew

Carol M Goodwin

Ian Gordon

Lady Anne Graham

Andrew Graham

Christopher J R Graham

Meriel and Stephen Greenwood

Philip Grimes

Ruth Grimshaw

Jean Hadwin

Mr S R Hall

Terence Hall

Gillian Hall

Adrian Hanks

Uncle Hariram

Anne Hartley

Helen

Sybil Hewitt

R J Hibbert

Alan Hill

Raymond Hill

Norman Hitchen

Helen Hocking

Kev Hodgkinson

Bethan Hook

Leslie Horton

Gladys Howarth

David Huxley

Peter A Jackson

Maura & Steve James

Jane

Jeannine

Karen & Colin Johnson

K Jolleys

Ken Jones

Irene Jones

Barry & Jane Keeran

Alec Kinghorn

The Lake Family

Wendy Lavelle

Mr J Layfield

Roger Lazenby

Christine Leith

Brian Leonard

Kenneth William Lynn

J E Mallinson

Anna Marsh

Brian Marshall

Mary & Angela

Nicholas Masheter

Tom Mason

Ian Matthewson

Monica Maxted Jones

Mrs S J McGee

Edna Mole

Catherine monkhouse

Andrew Morgan

Constance Mary Morley

Dr Christopher Morris

Robert Morton

Sir Kenneth Murray

Kevin Mylchreest

Bill Nickson

Paul Nickson

Robert Nickson

Margaret O'Neil

Tom Orr

Audrey Owen

Mr M Pamphilon

Trevor & Diane Park

Pauline

Walter Richard Payne

Cliff Pearse

Dr David Pearson

Alexander Richard Peel

Margaret Pinder

Malcolm Pitts

Derek Porter (Holker School)

Rona Pridding

Roy Pryor

The Read Family

Renée

Kathryn Richardson

Rick, Benn & Vicky the invisible flock

Irene & Peter Riley

Ruth Roberts

Catherine Roberts

Susan Robinson

Olive Robinson

Carl Rogerson

Margaret P Rowe

Phillip Saunders

Jean & Tony Sawrey

Christopher Schofield

Bryan Schofield

David Selmes

Ruth Shoesmith

Garth J Smart

The Late Margaret Smith

Christine Smith

J V Smith

Tony Smith

Arnold Staples

George Stephenson

F R A Stirk

Roy Stubbs

Sue & Tony

TV Sykes, Dacre, Cumbria

Barbara Tankard

David Tattersall

In loving Memory of
Dean Thompson

Ann Thorington

Hilary Thwaites

Alan Tomlinson

David Turvey

Garry Turvey

Brooke J VanHinsbergh

Bill Wakefield

George R Walsh

Diane Ward

Ian J Ward (Thorner)

Ella Ann Webb

Don Webster

Oliver M Westall

Ruth Westall

Joyce White

Cynthia & Derrick Whiting

David H Williams

Robert John Winter

Roger Winterburn

Jacqueline Susan Woodward

Paul Wright

Mr Ted Yates

Also available from Great Northern Books:

GREAT YORKSHIRE BEER

by Leigh Linley

THE LAST DAYS OF SCOTTISH STEAM

by Peter Tuffrey

featuring photography from the Bill Reed Collection

DAUGHTER OF BLUEBIRD

by Gina Campbell

THE GREAT BOOK OF YORKSHIRE PUDDING

THE GREAT BOOK OF RHUBARB!

THE GREAT BOOK OF TEA

by Elaine Lemm

ROSEMARY SHRAGER'S

YORKSHIRE BREAKFASTS

TOP TEN OF YORKSHIRE

A cornucopia of fascinating facts about God's Own County

by Mike Fox

Visit www.greatnorthernbooks.co.uk

Follow us on Twitter: @gnbooks